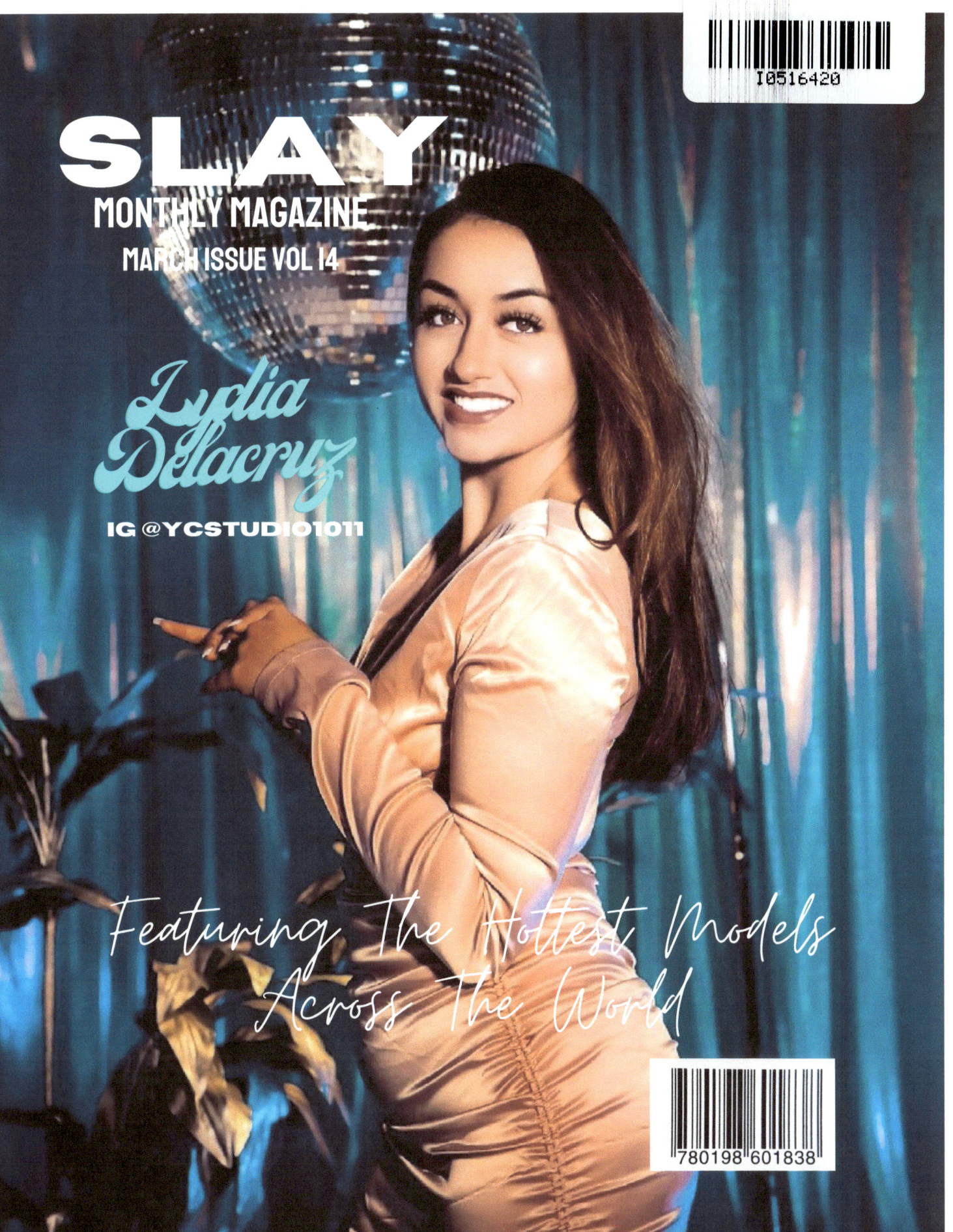

IN THIS ISSUE

Lydia Belacruz
Photographer
IG @ycstudio1011
Dress: Blaque Barbie Boutique
Hmua Lydia Belacruz

Lakrisha S Davidson Aka Kween Kree
IG: @iamkweenkree
Photographer: Calvin Davidson @ Cali-Cal Creations
@cali_cal_creations

Shay Renee
IG: @thereal_shayrenee
Photographer Ray Coleman
IG: @rcoleman_photos

Stephanie Johnson Rice
Photographer: Brandon J Geer
IG: @big_vimages

Tigerlily Rose
Photographer: Joshua Manning with Virtual Instinct Photography

Carla dawes
Model IG: carladawes
Photographer: Jess leek
Photographer IG: mjsphotography123

Krix Hinton
Photographer: Wade Hinton with W.H. Media

Mckaylee Hernandez
Photographer: Troy Ritchie LN Beach Photography

MIKE THA MODEL
IG: @mikethamodel88
Photographer: @imperialoptics
Brand: @bosuh_way

Julian Valerio & Kassandra Perozoo
IG: @kravekonflict IG: @chikiichikii23
Photographer: Ray Coleman
IG: @rcoleman_photos

MONTHLY MAGAZINE

Onyx
FB: Beautifully Scarred Onyx Model Page
Ig: beautifullyscarred_onyx
Photographer: Kevin Beck Bombshell Exclusive Inc
FB: Kevin Beck
Ig: bombshellmodelcommunity

SecretAsia
Photo Credit- Aktive_shooter_photography
Edit- Aktive_shooter_photography
Location- Des Moines, Iowa

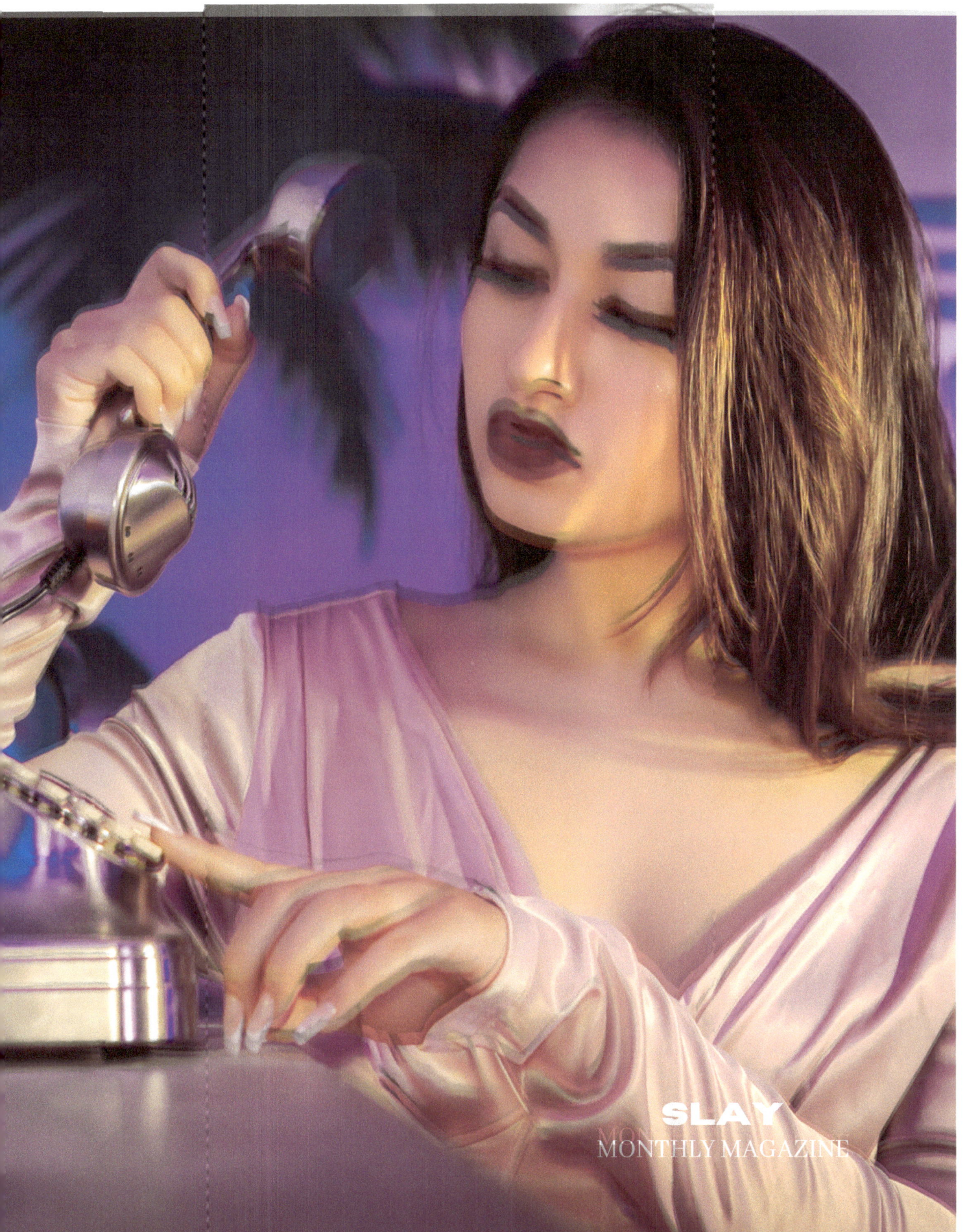

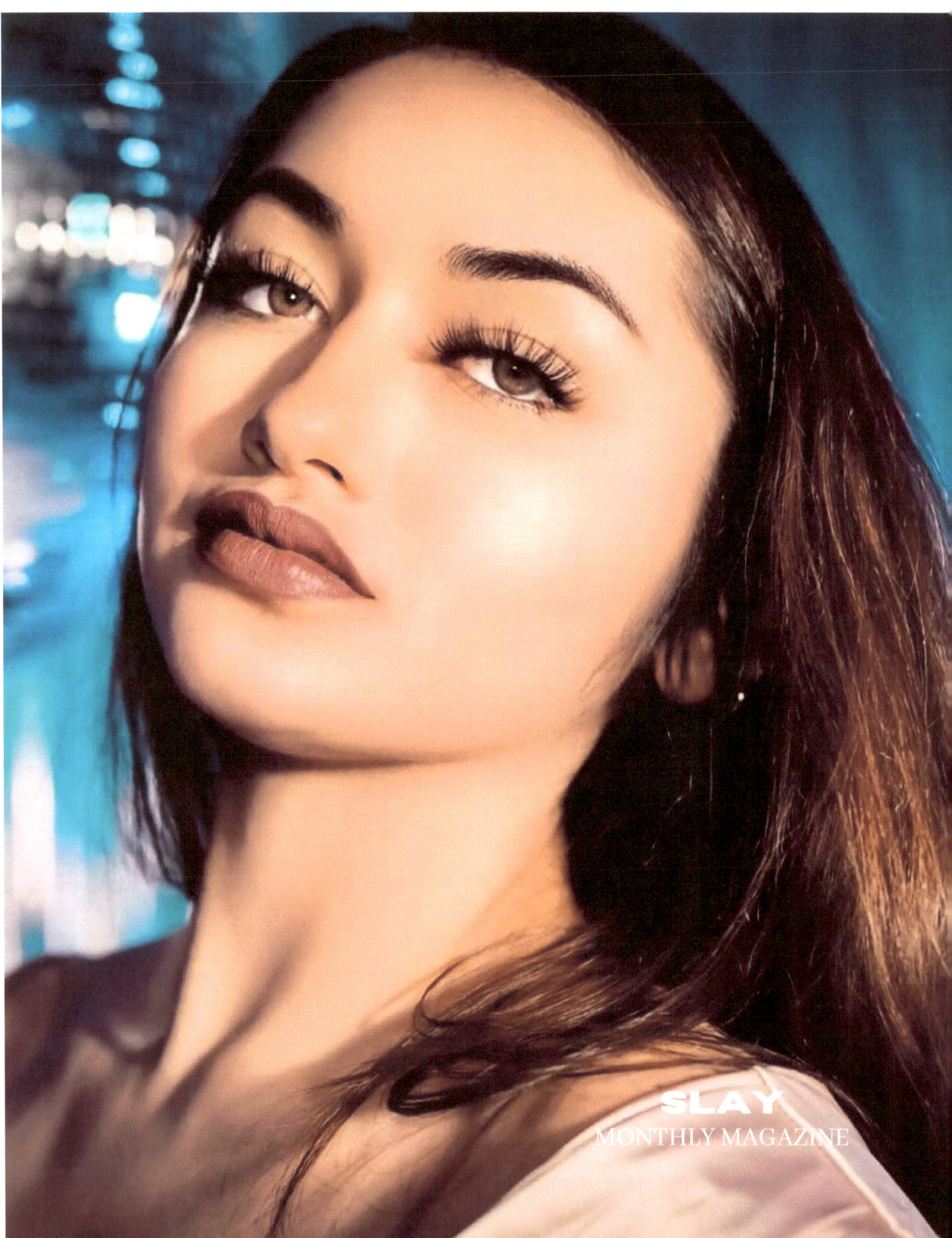

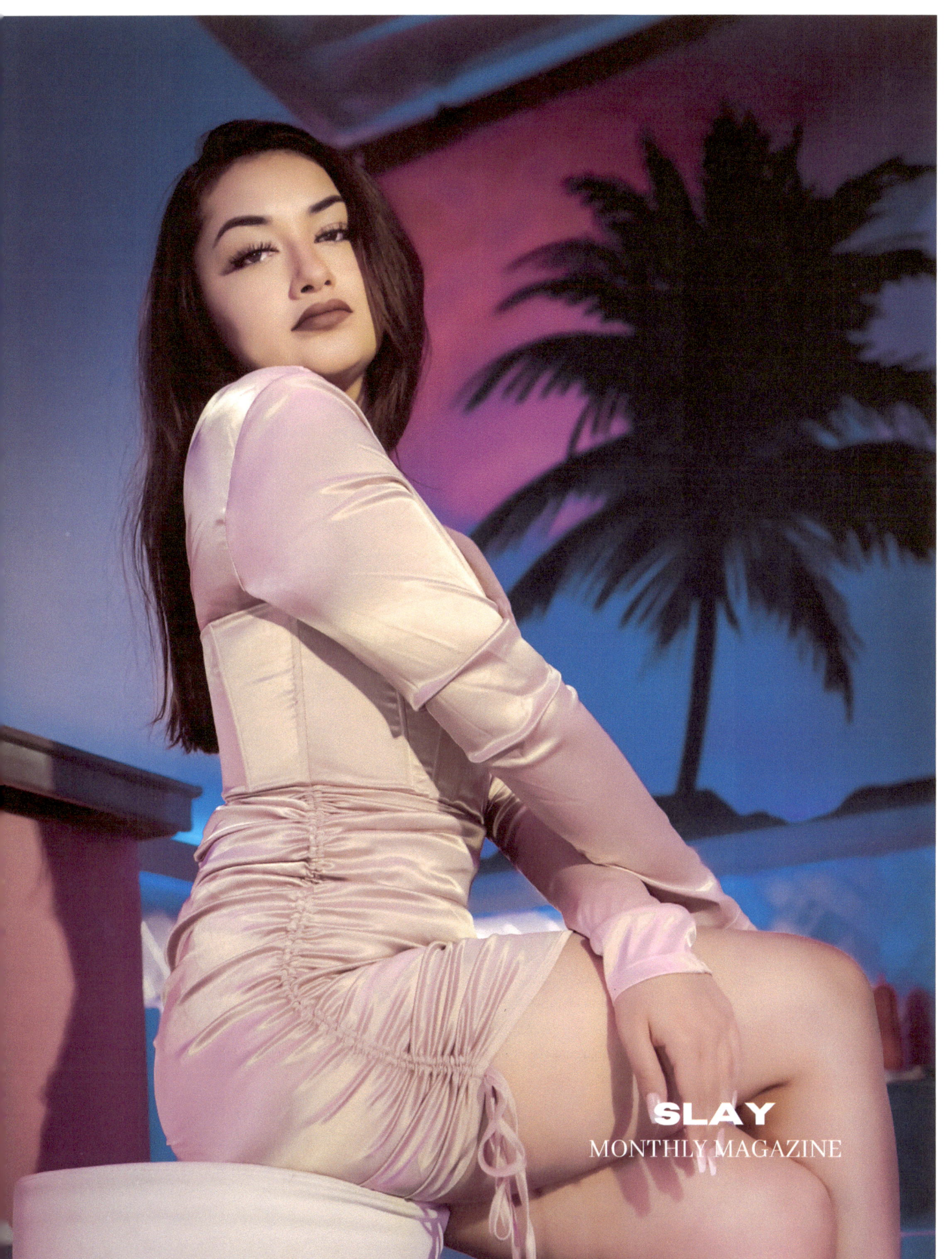

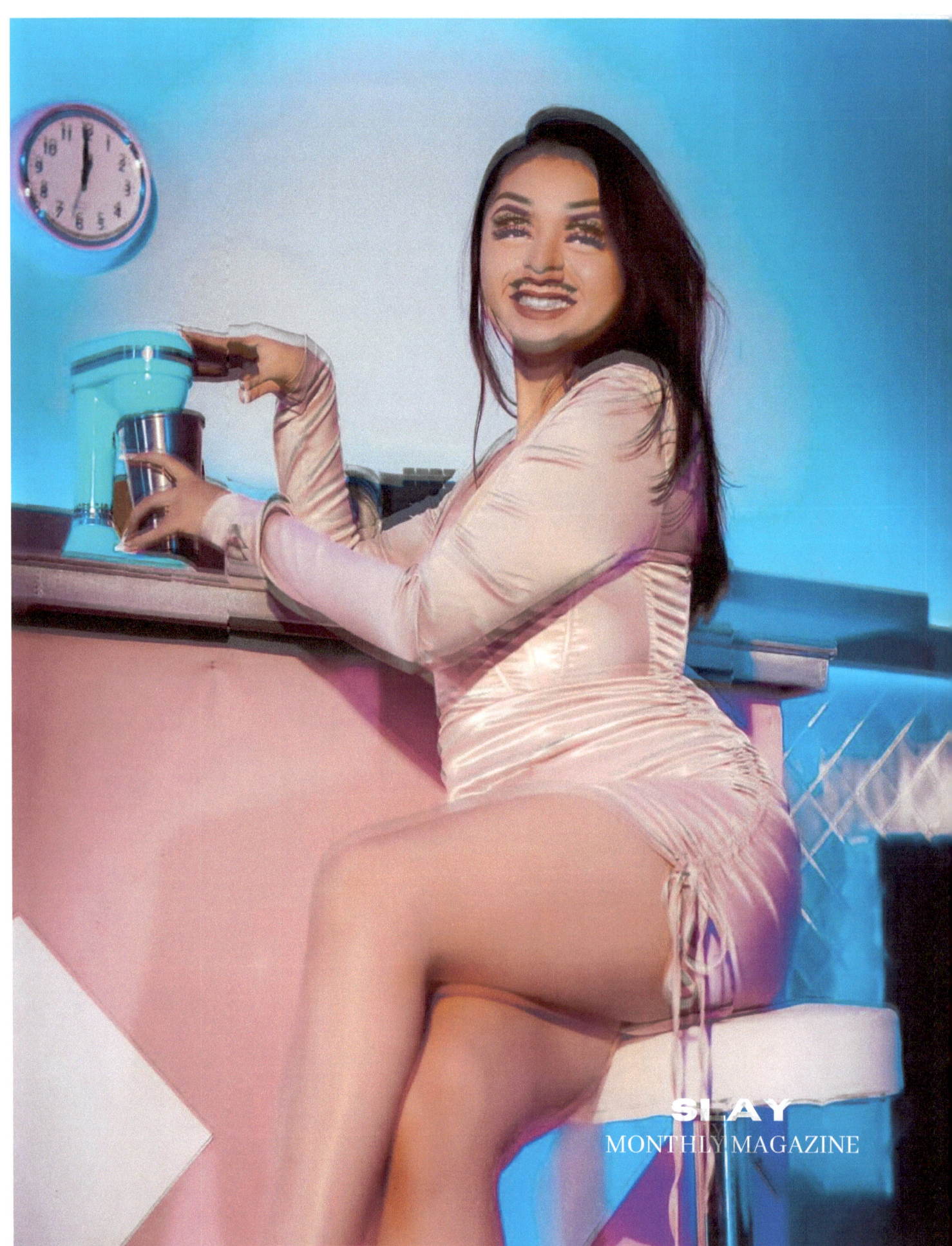

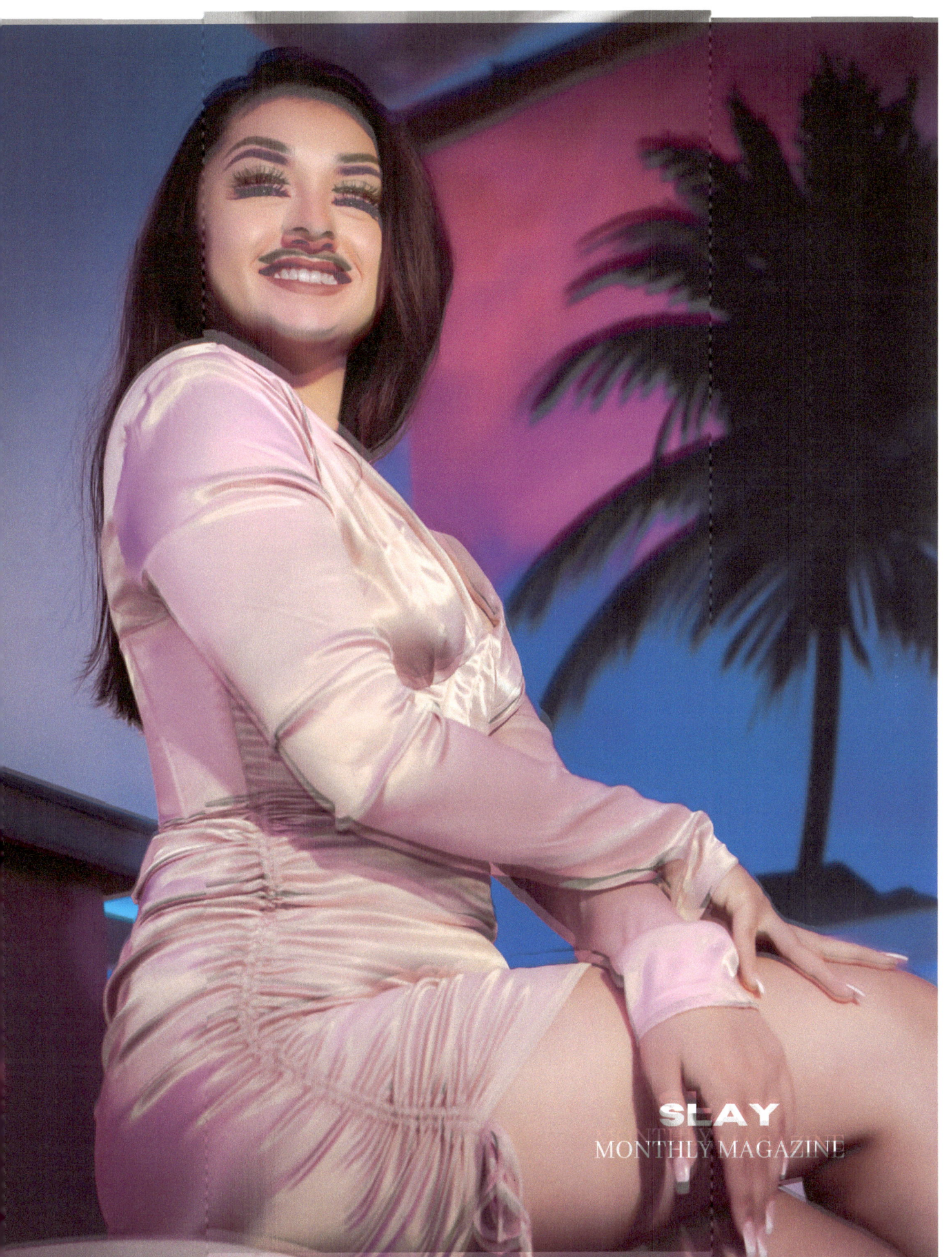

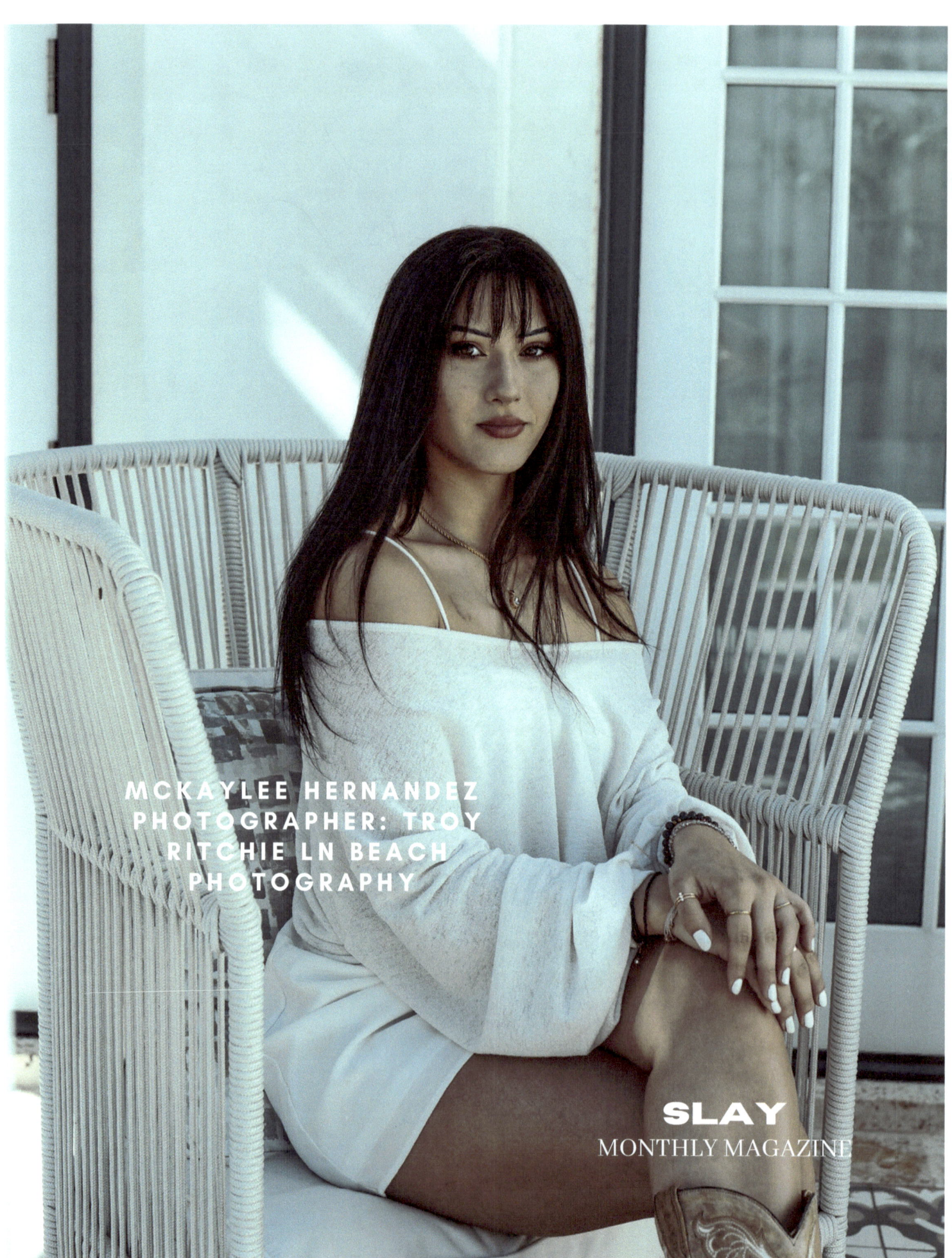

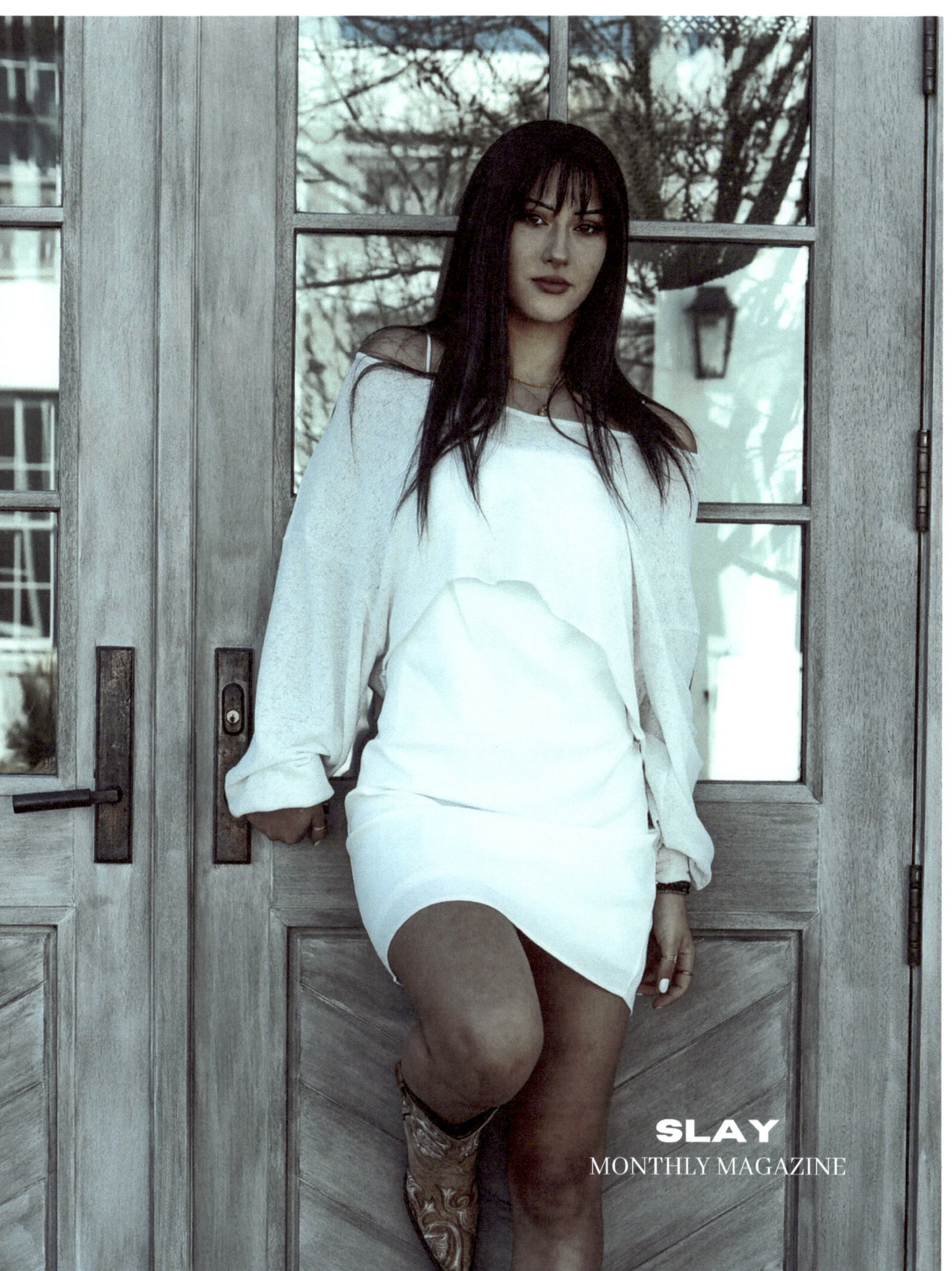

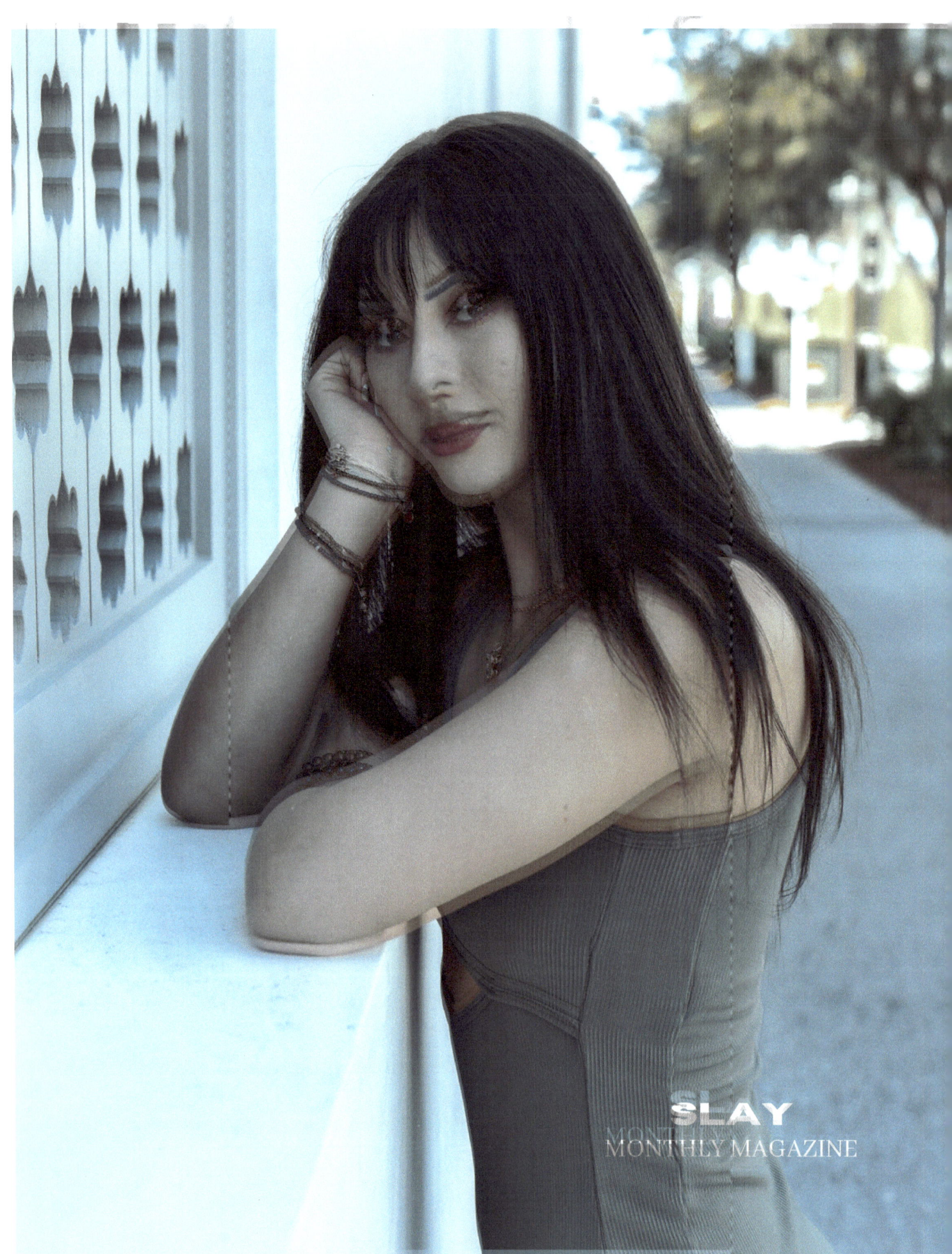

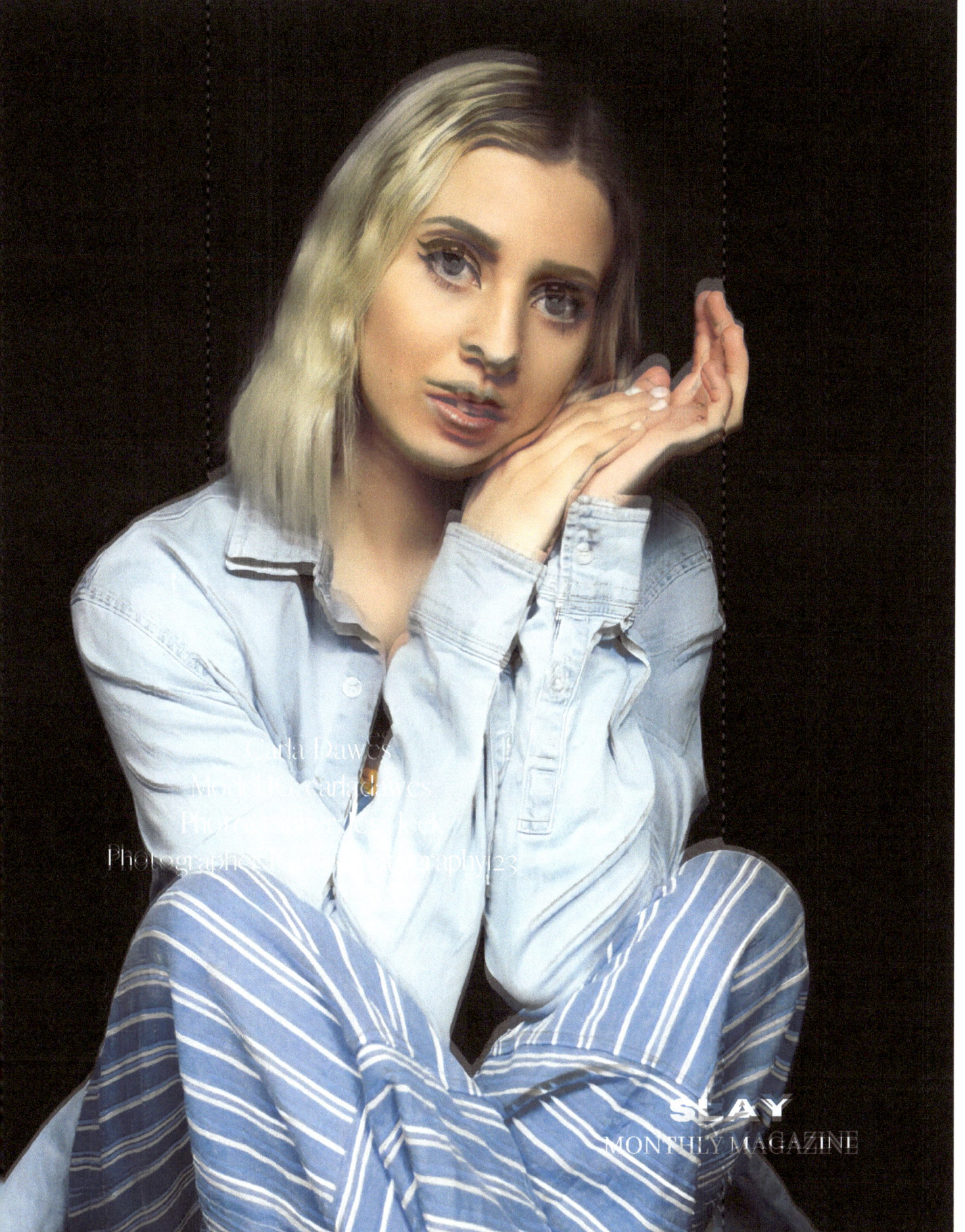

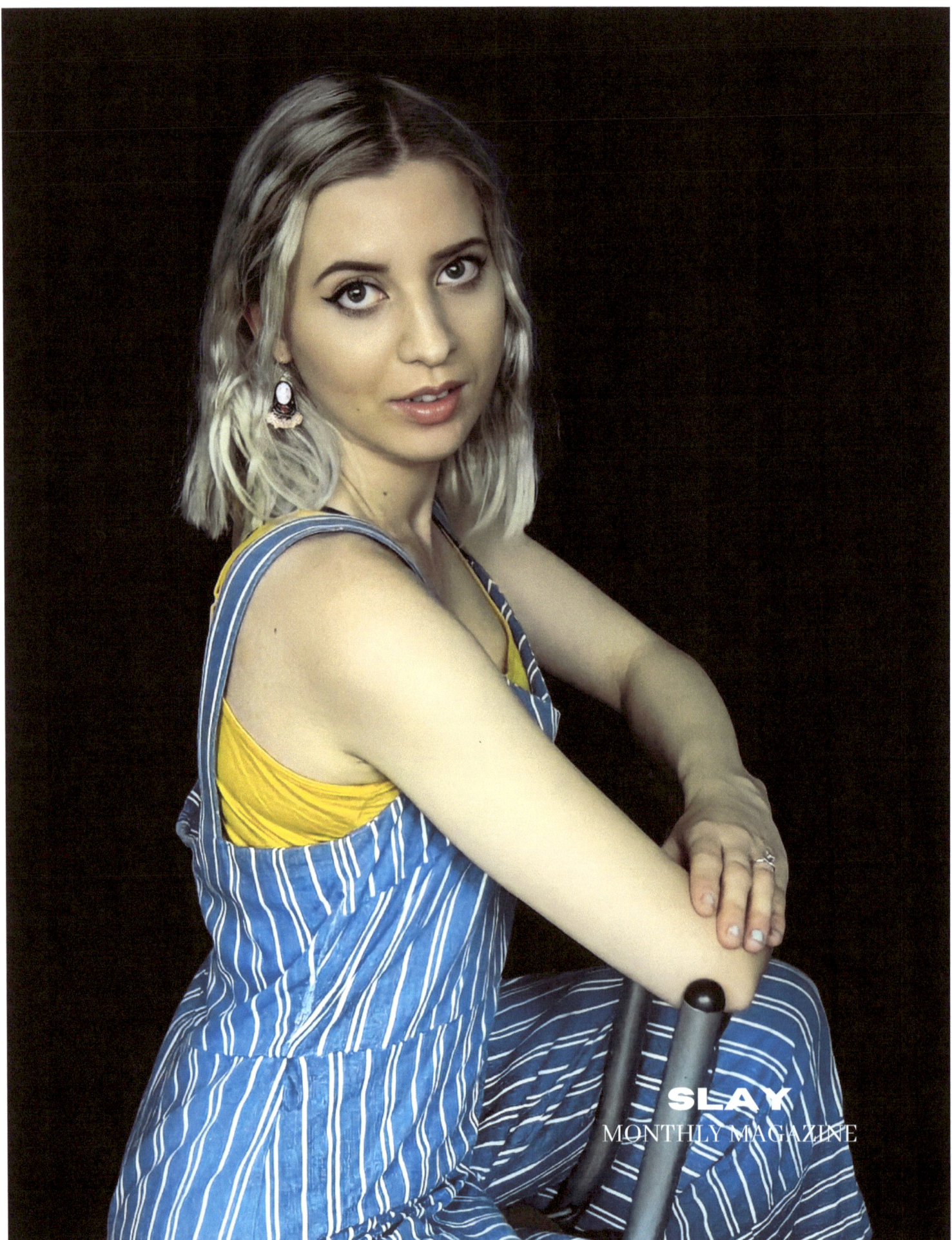

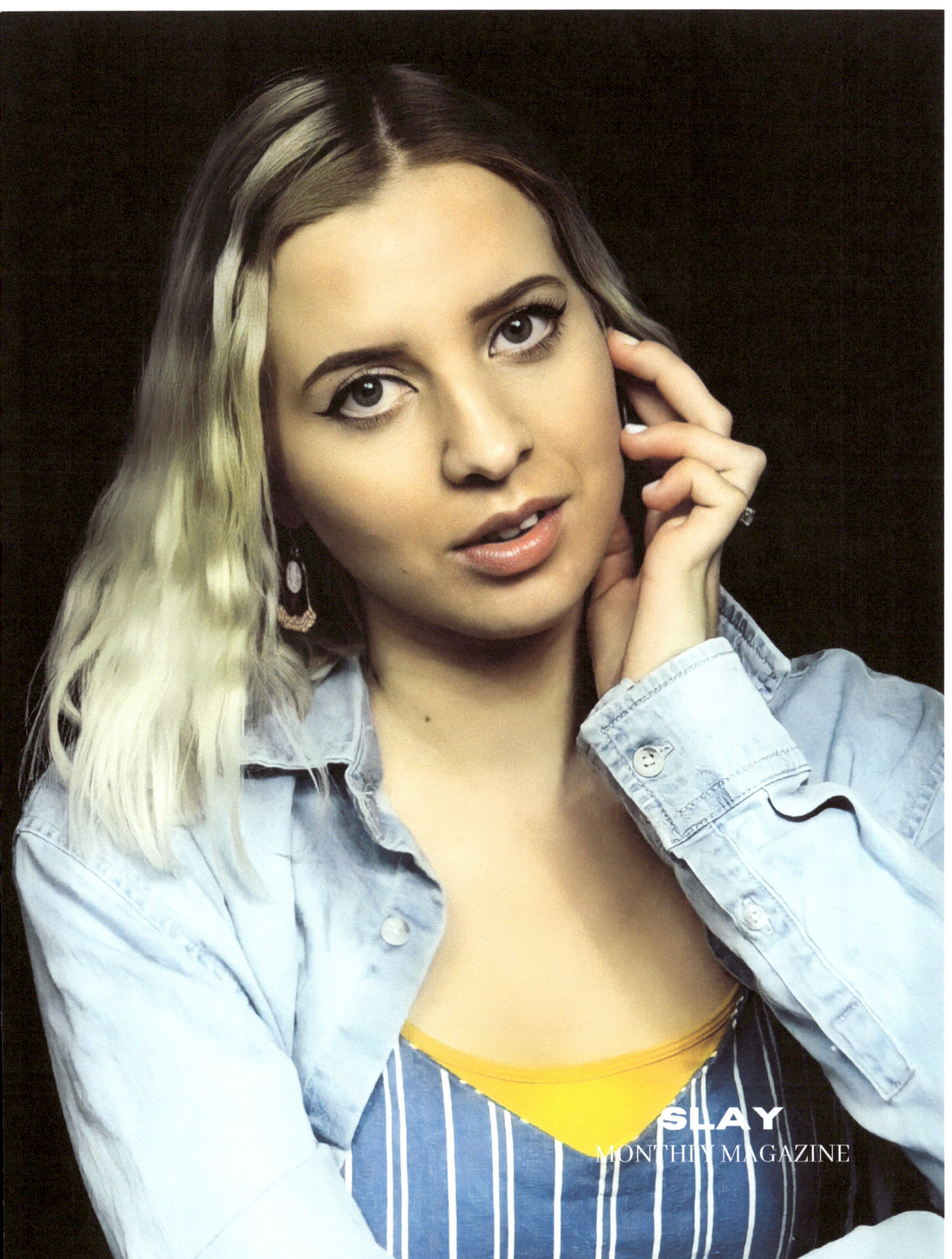

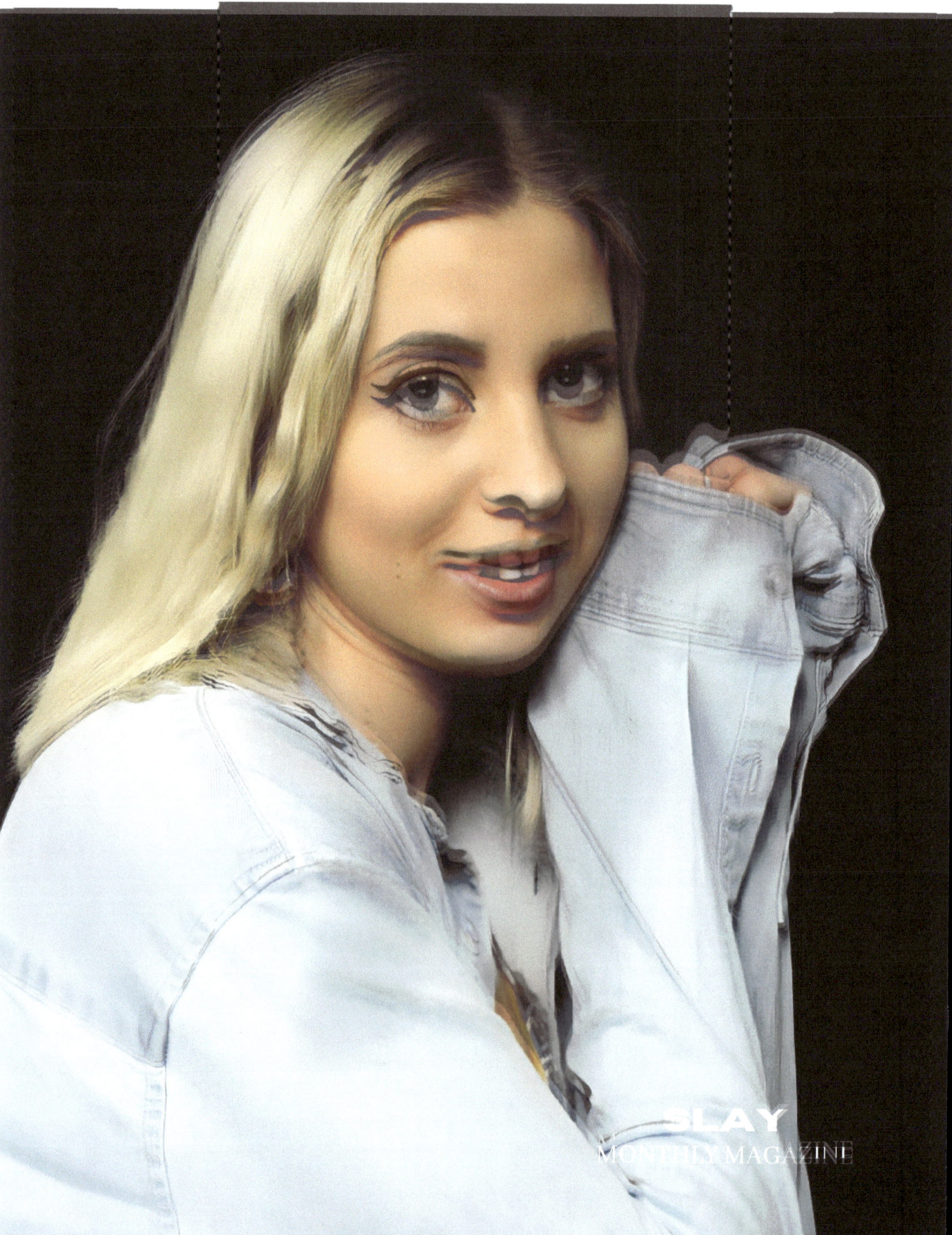

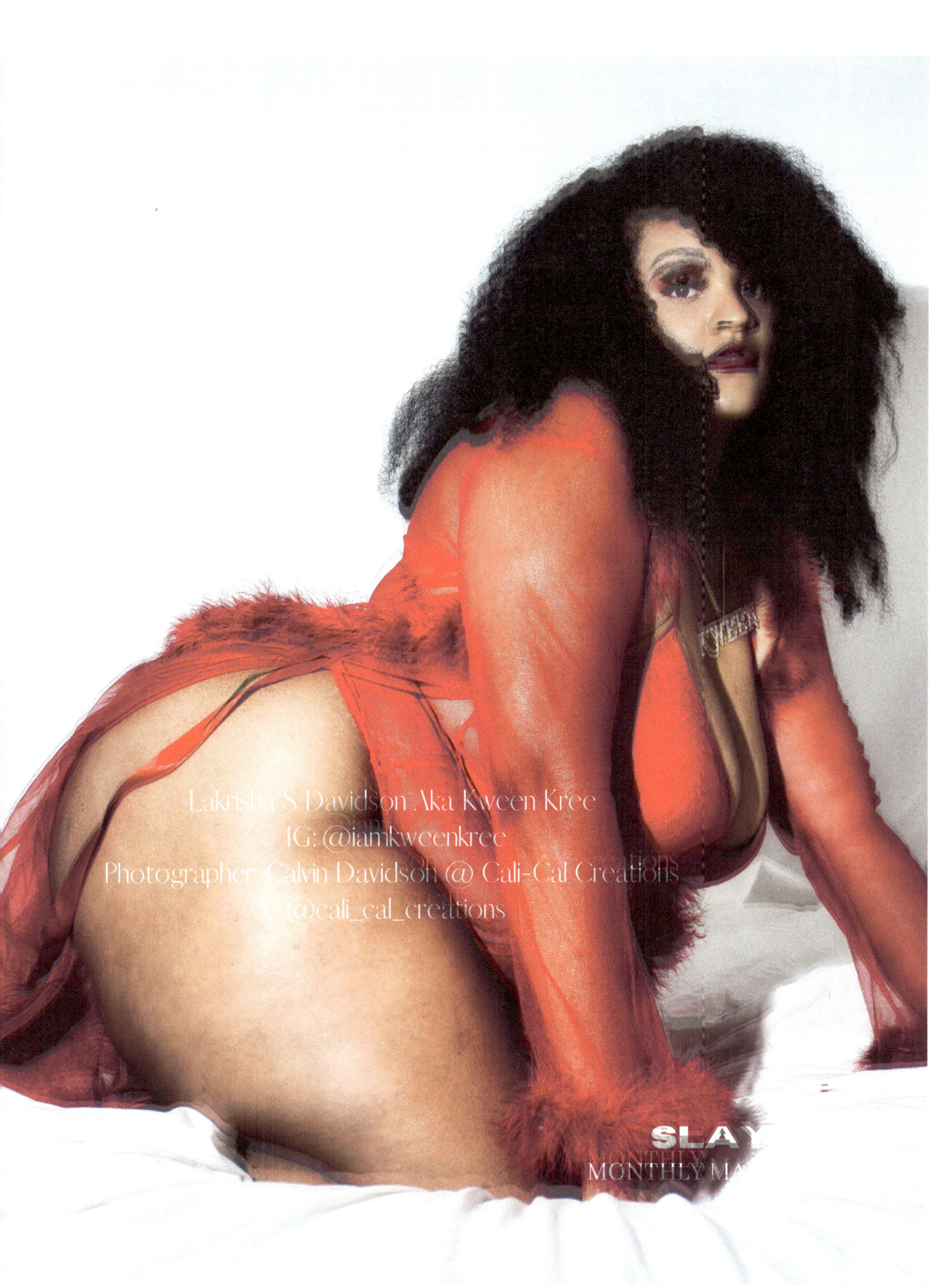

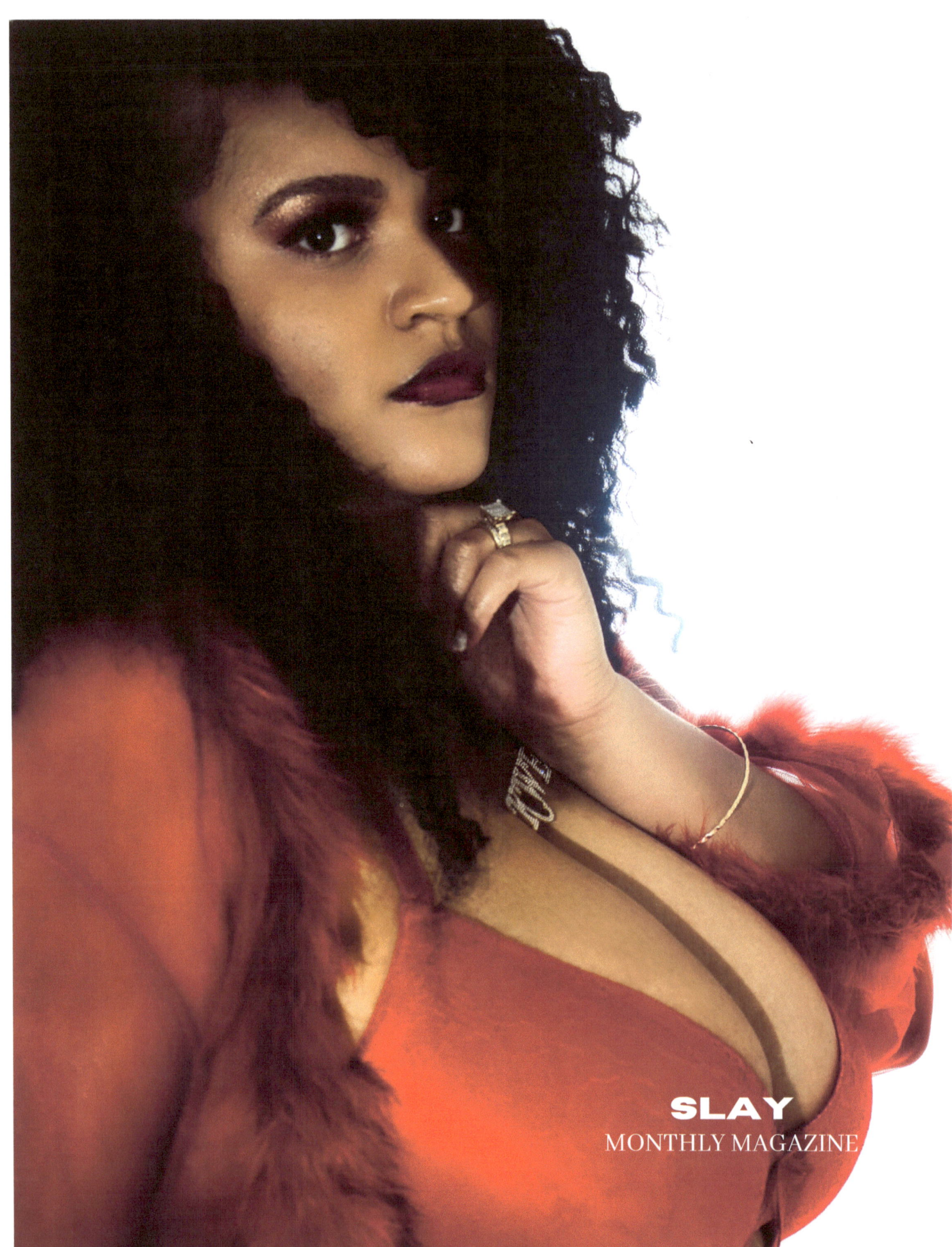

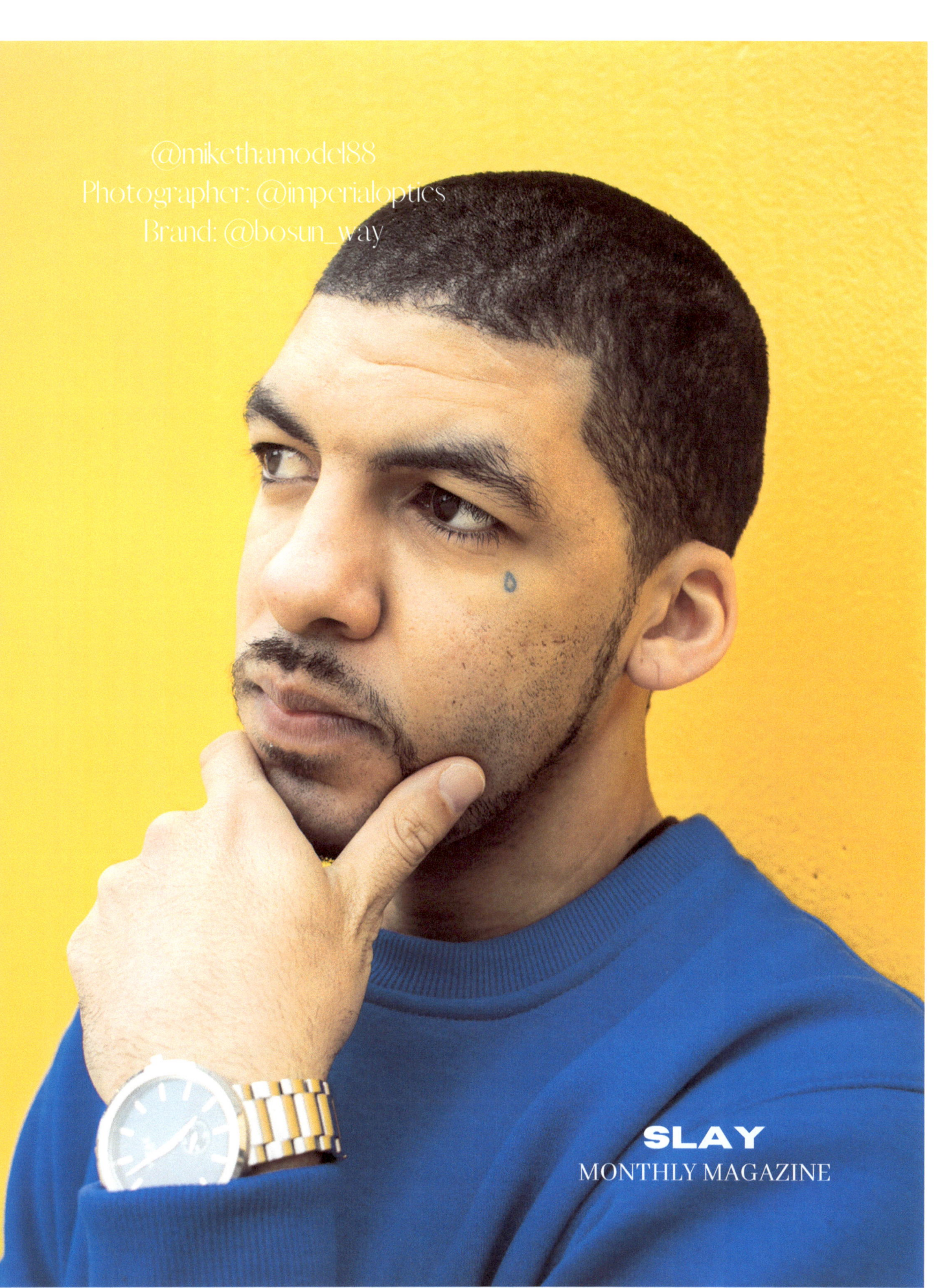

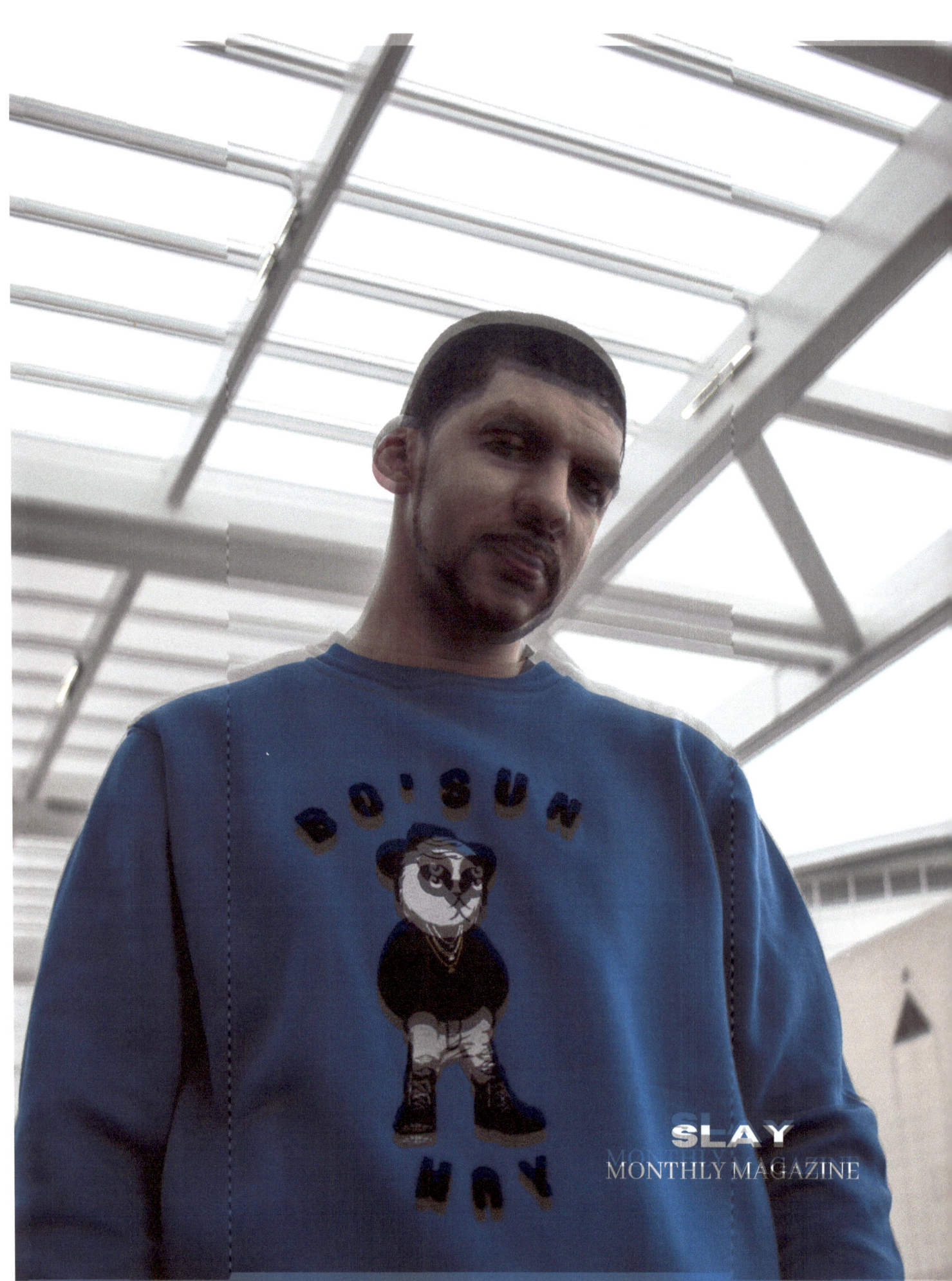

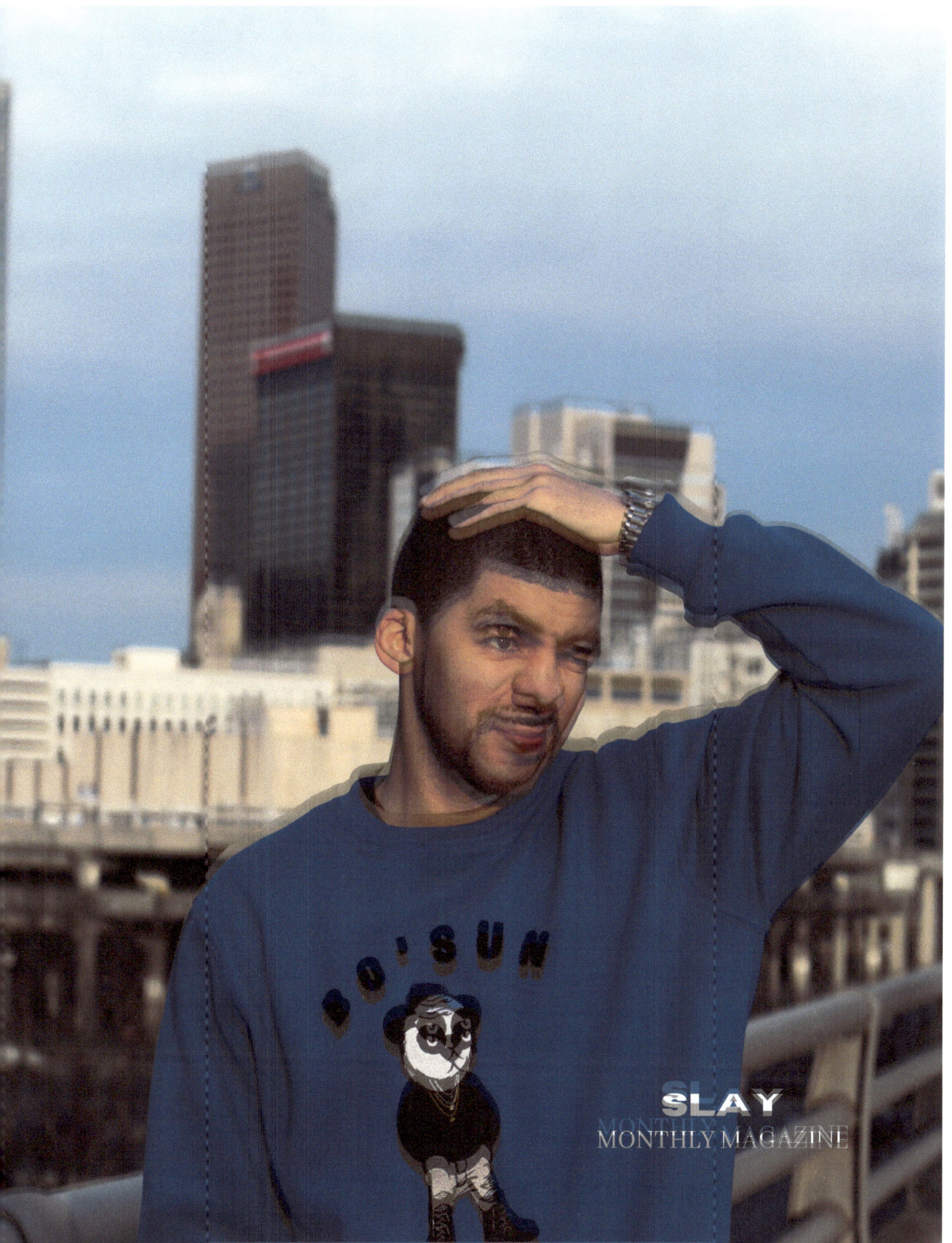

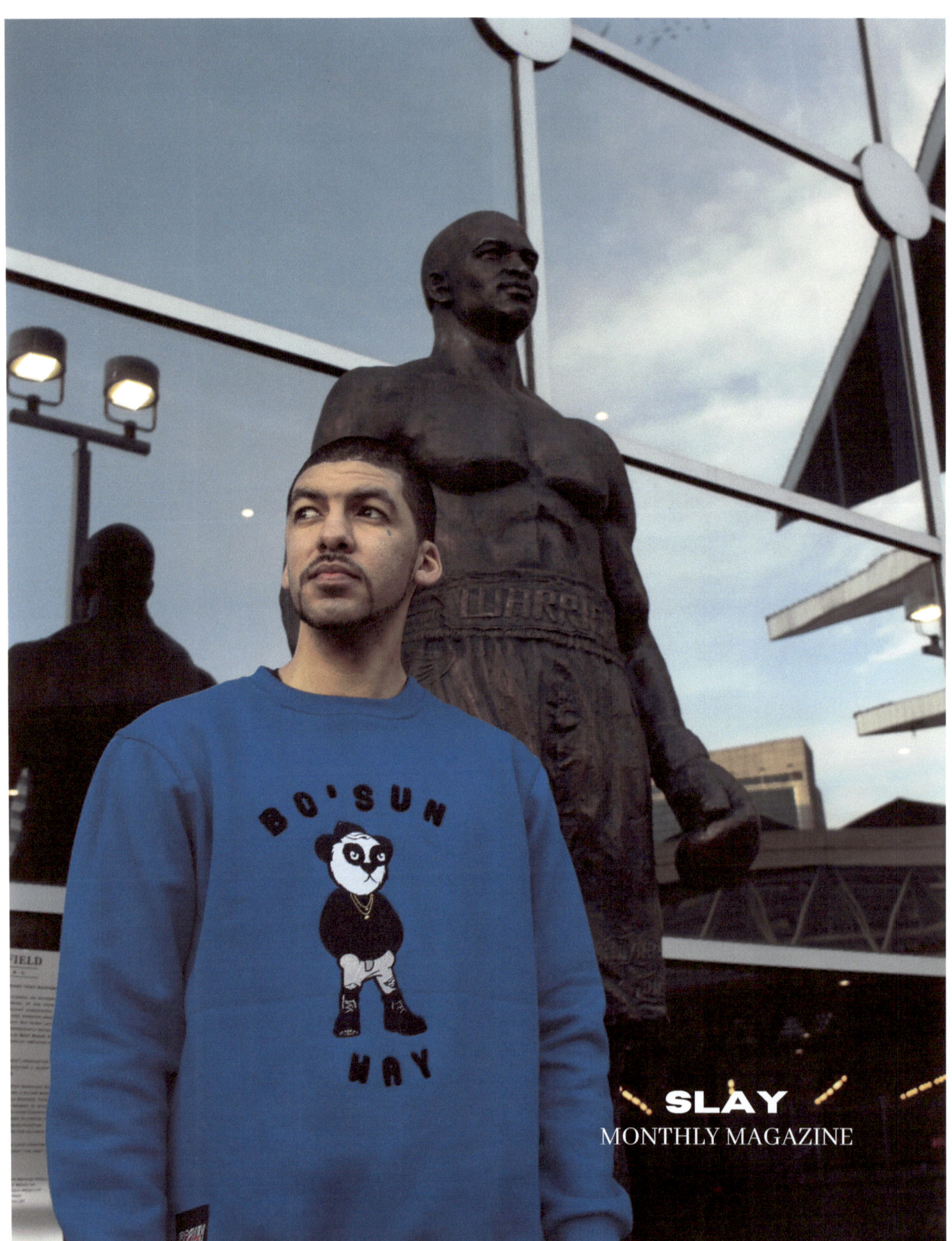

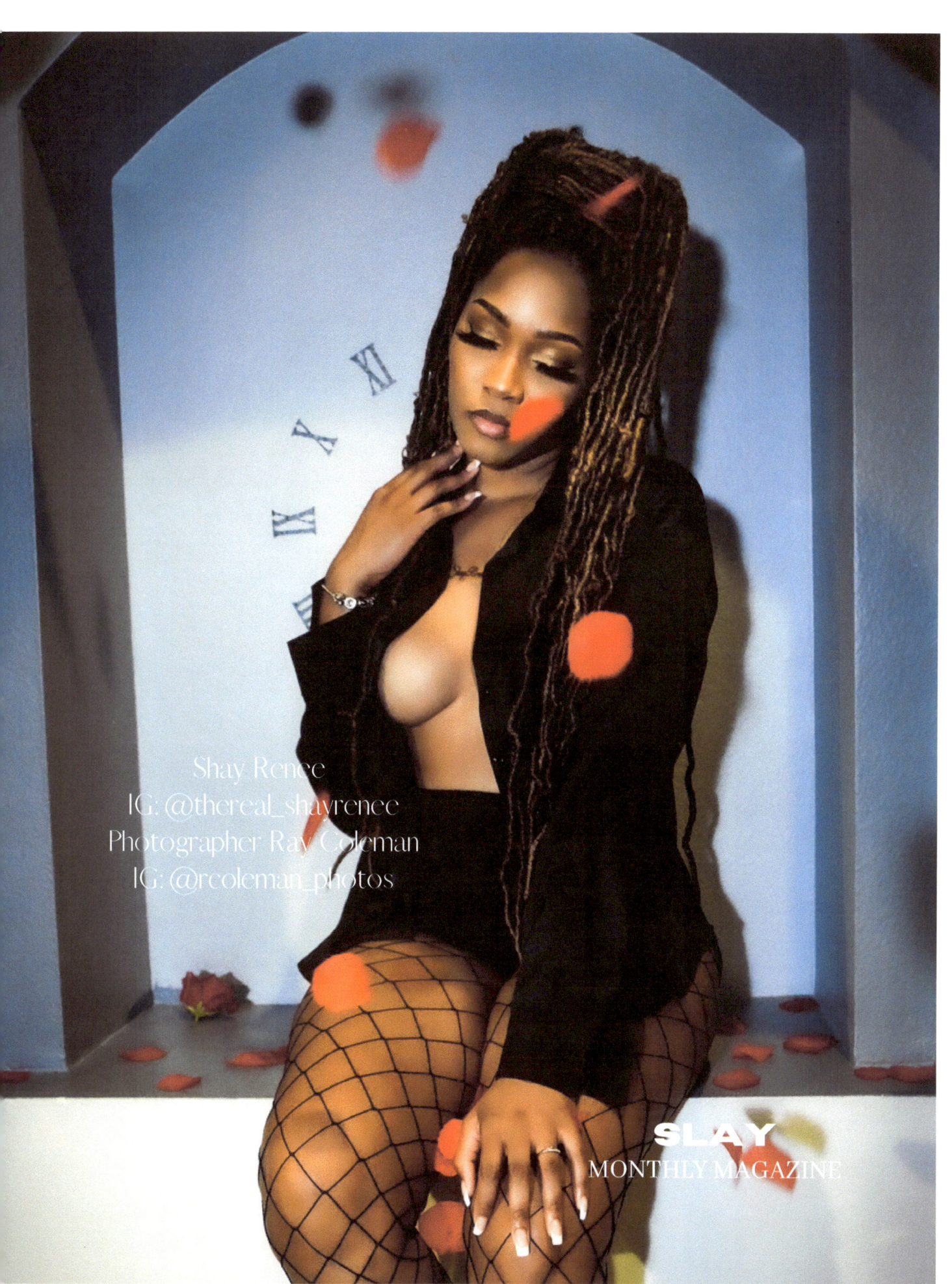

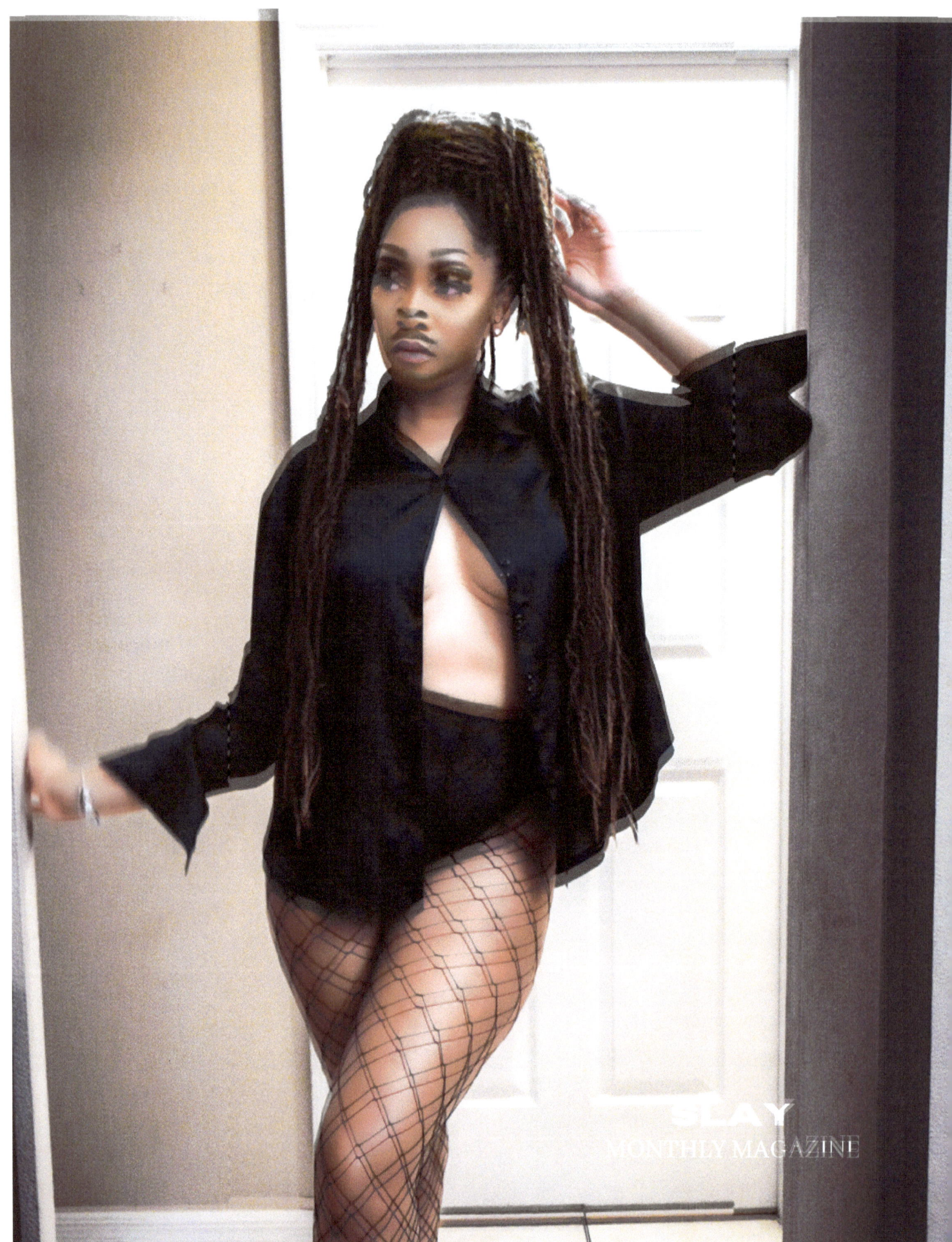

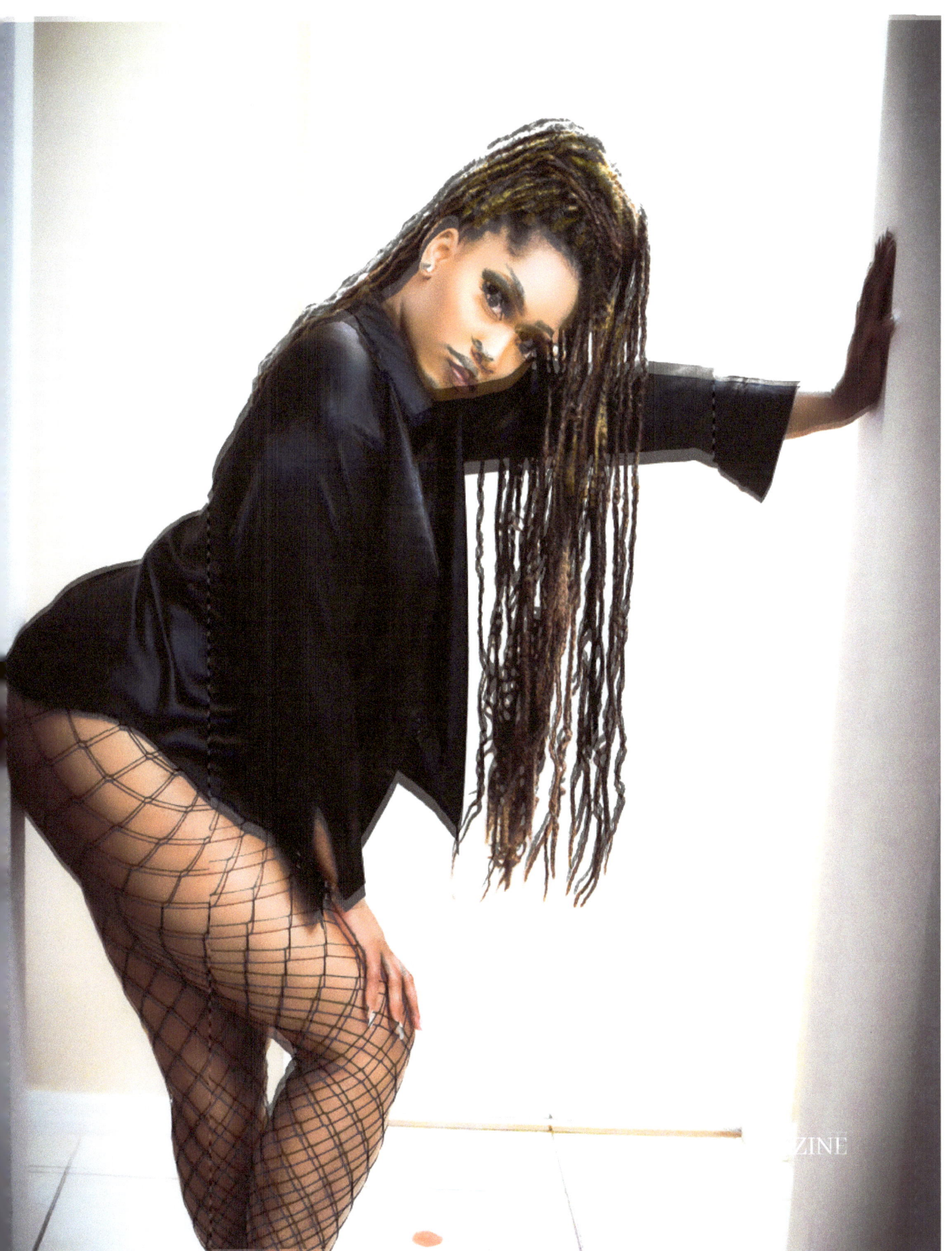

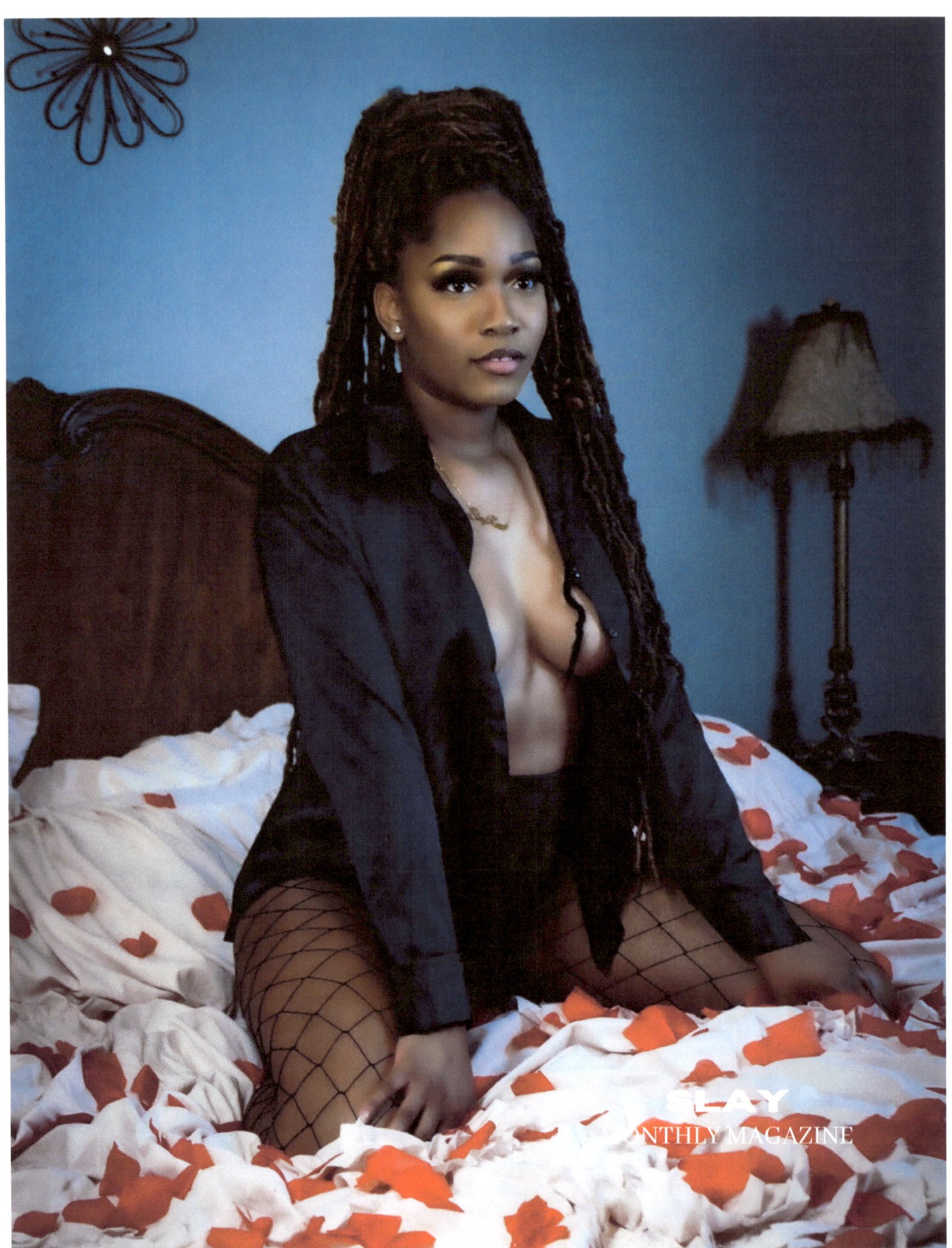

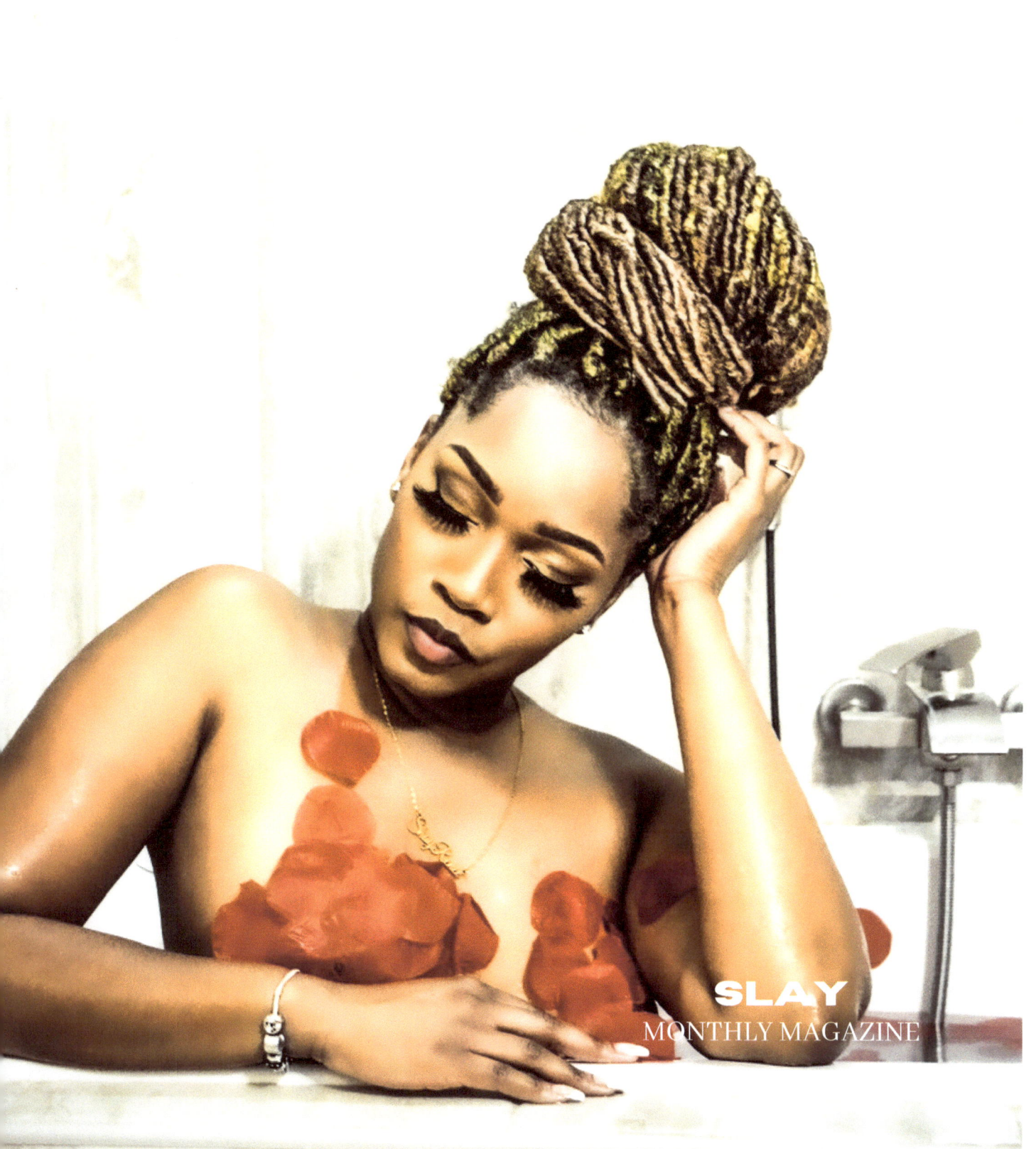

SLAY
MONTHLY MAGAZINE

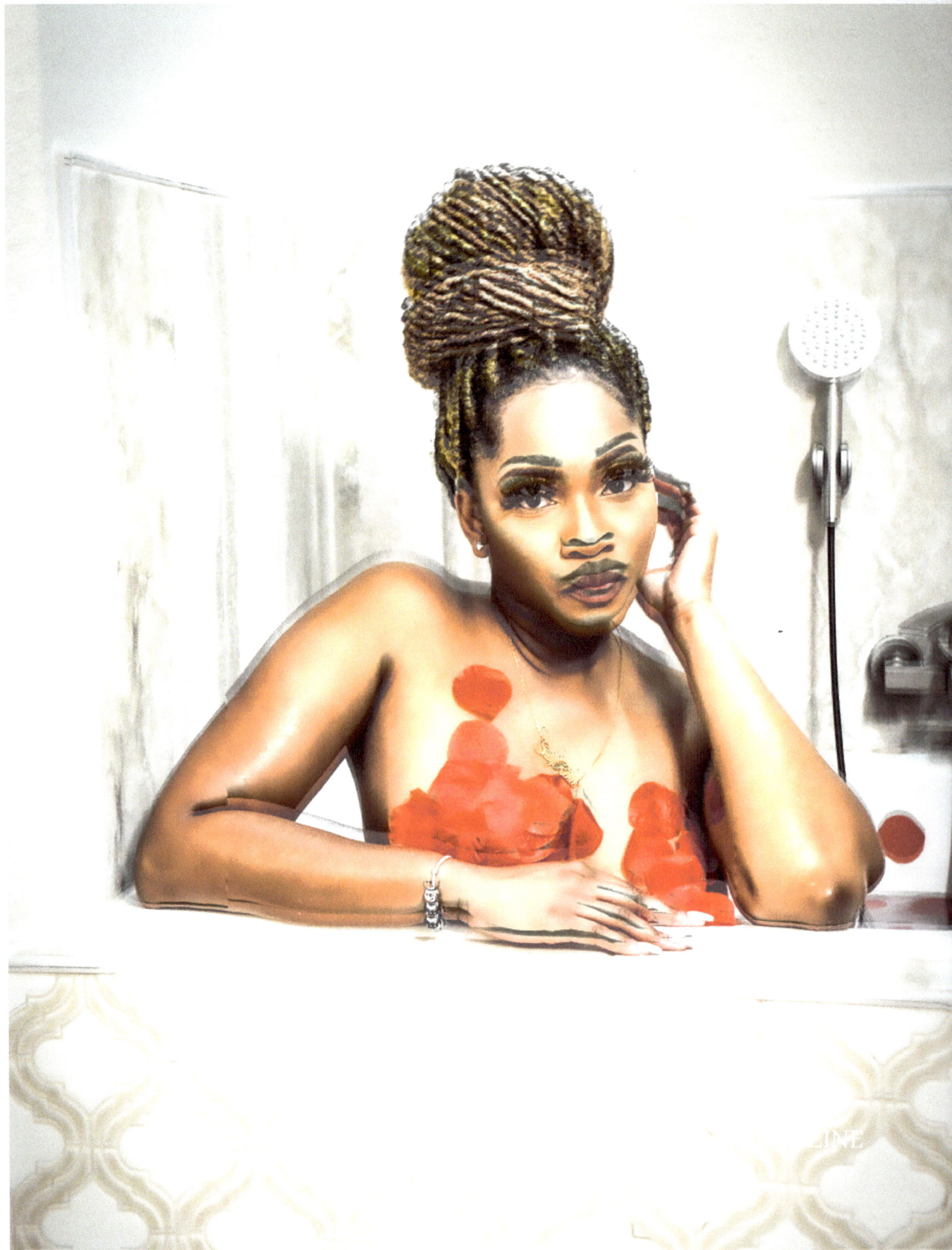

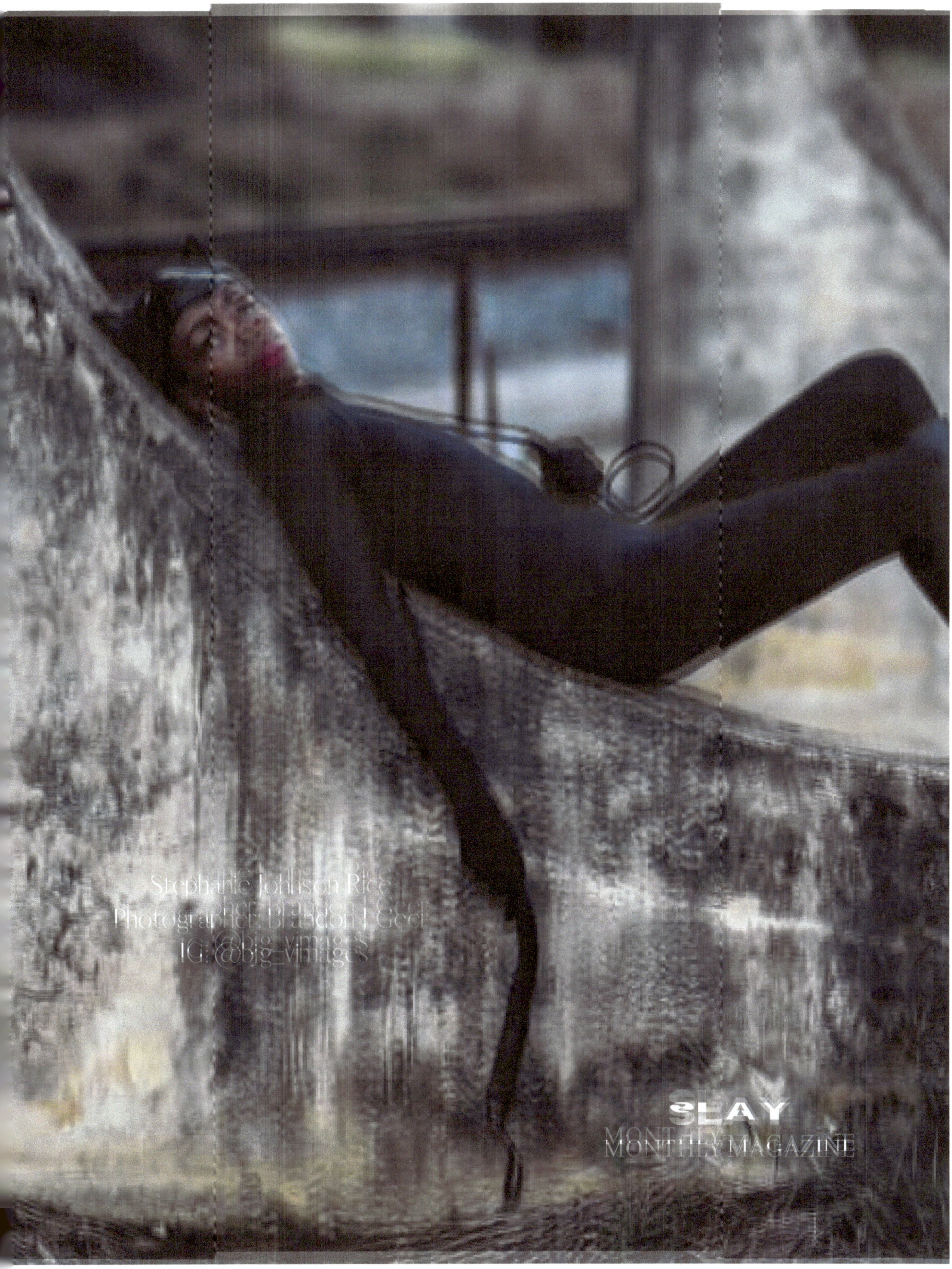

Stephanie Johnson-Rice
Photographer: Brandon Geter
IG: @big_vimages

SLAY
MONTHLY MAGAZINE

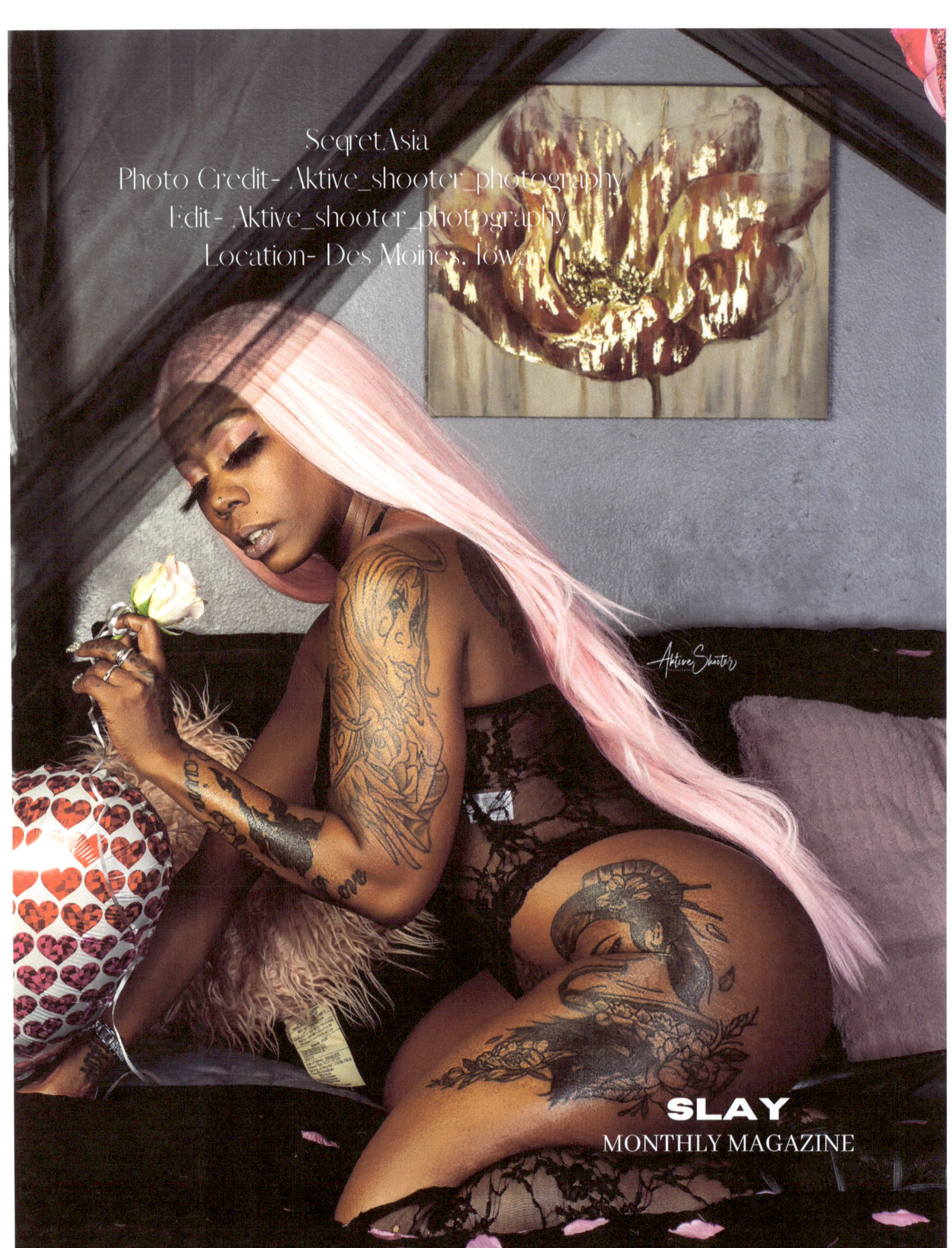

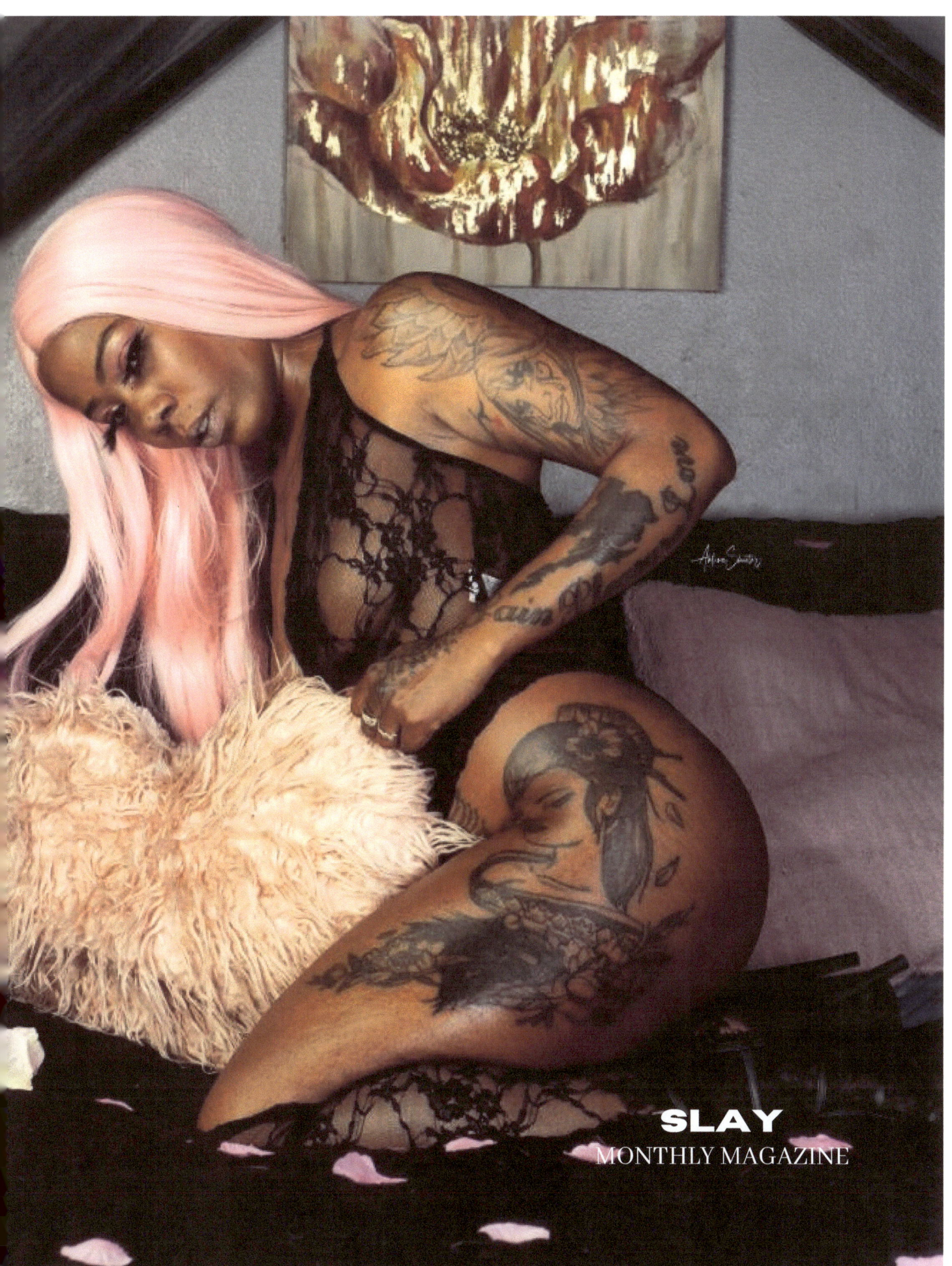

SLAY
MONTHLY MAGAZINE

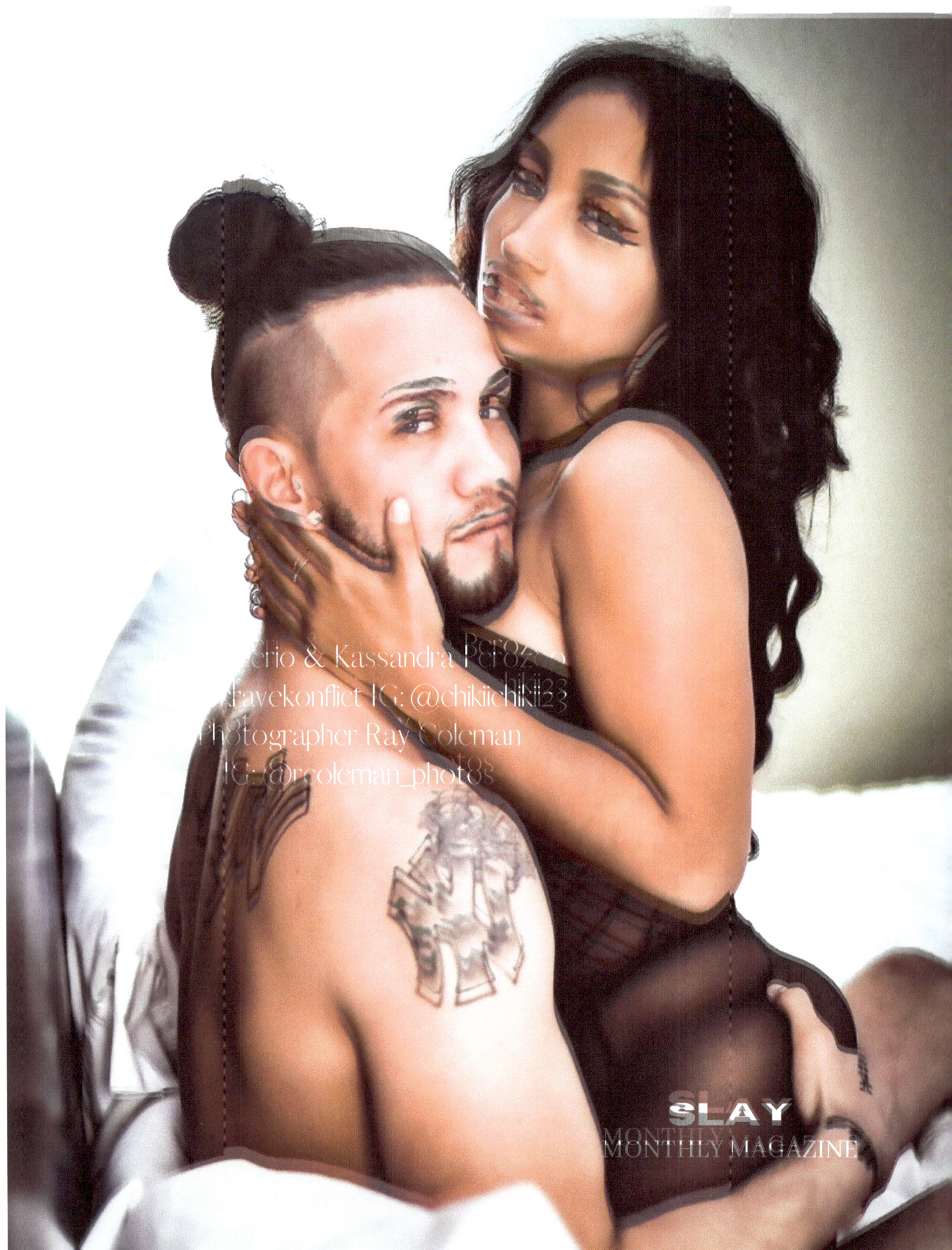

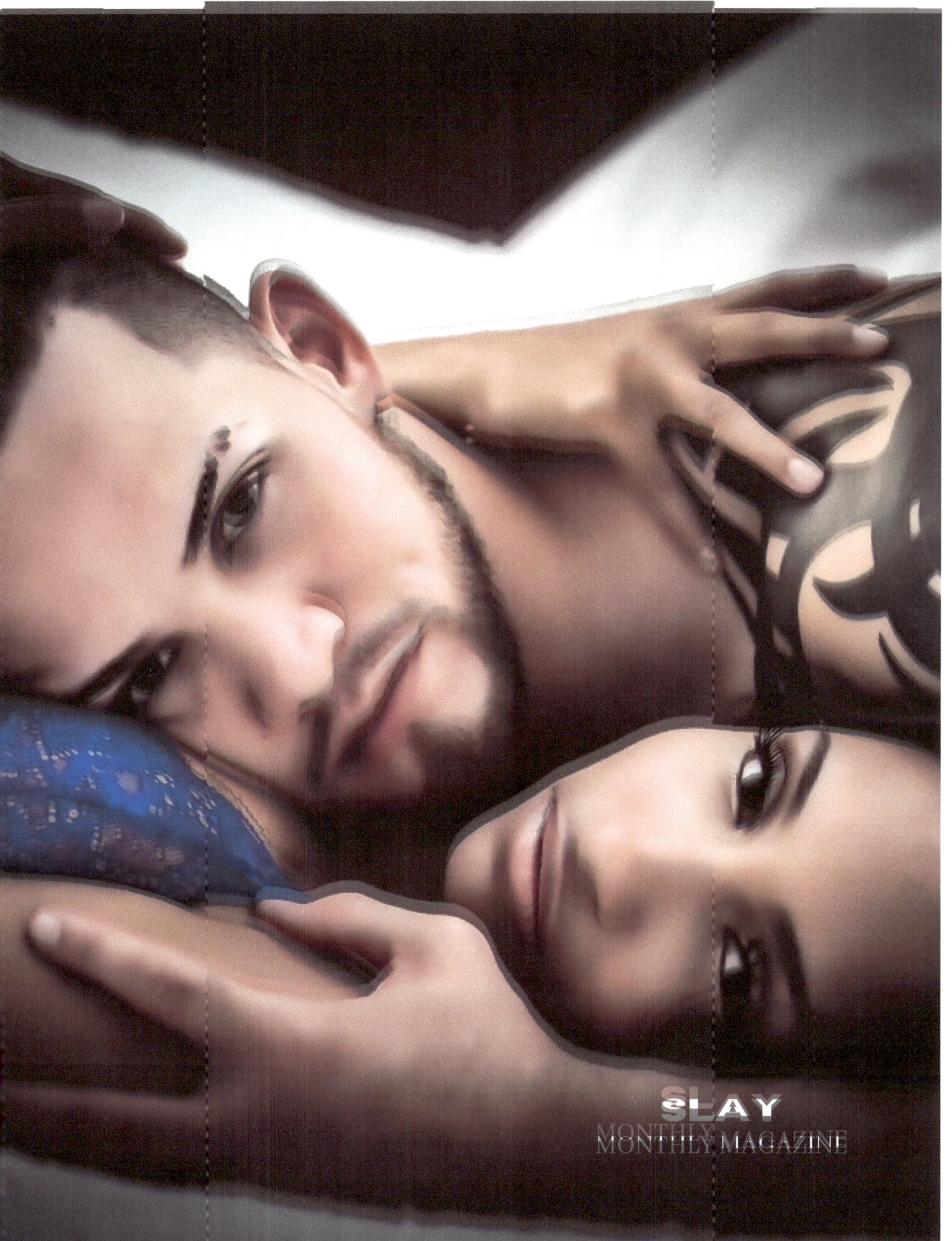

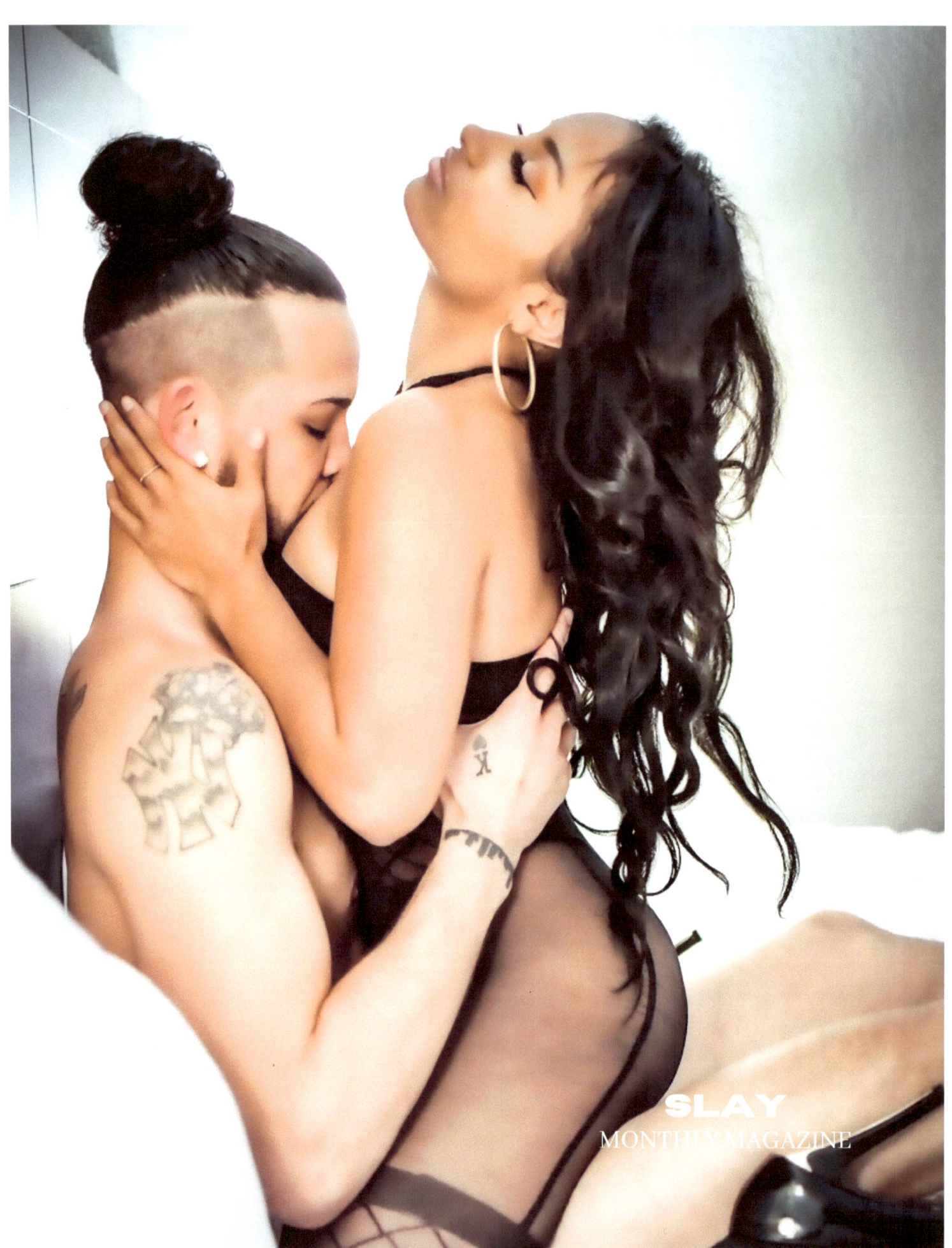

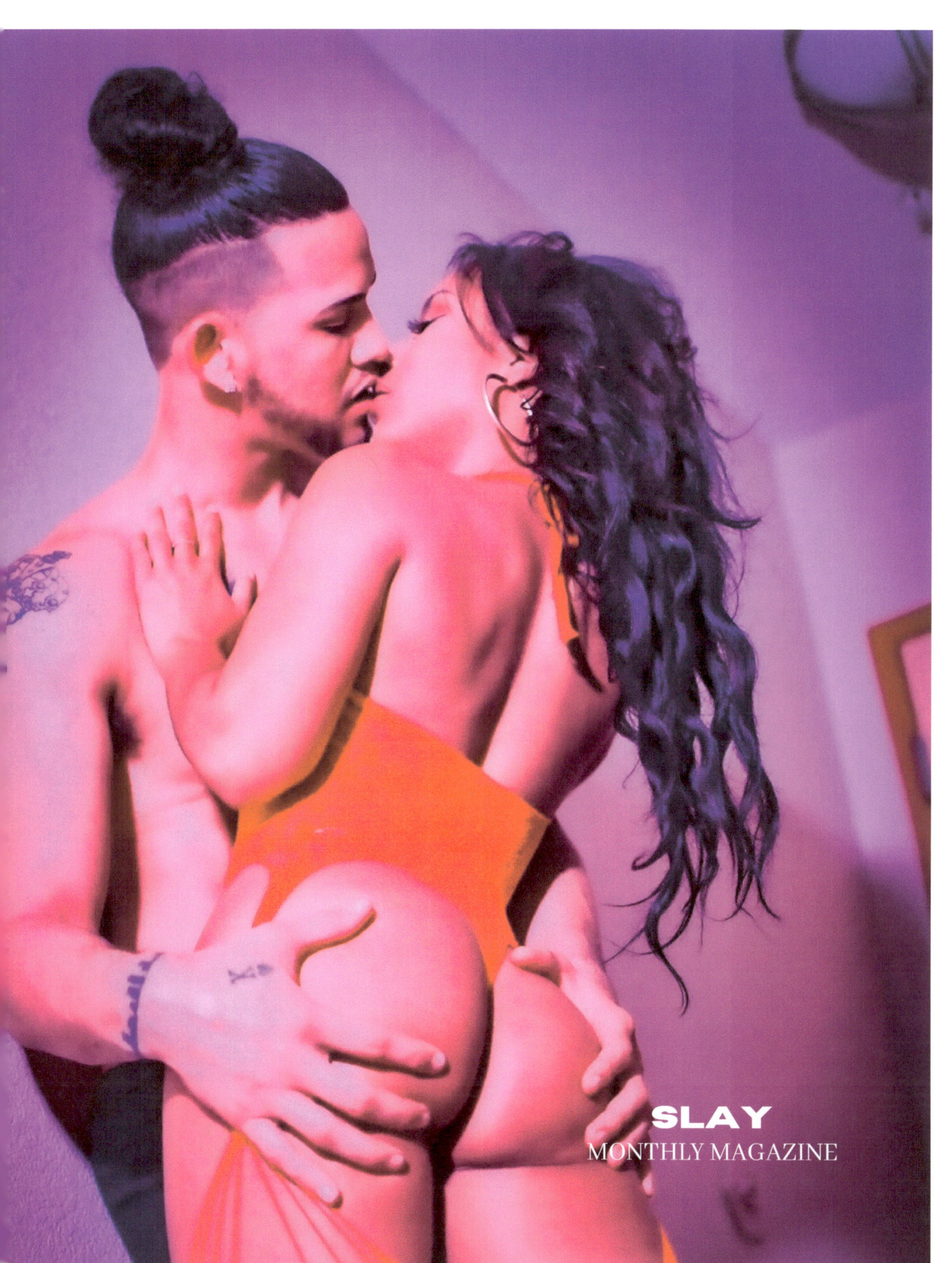

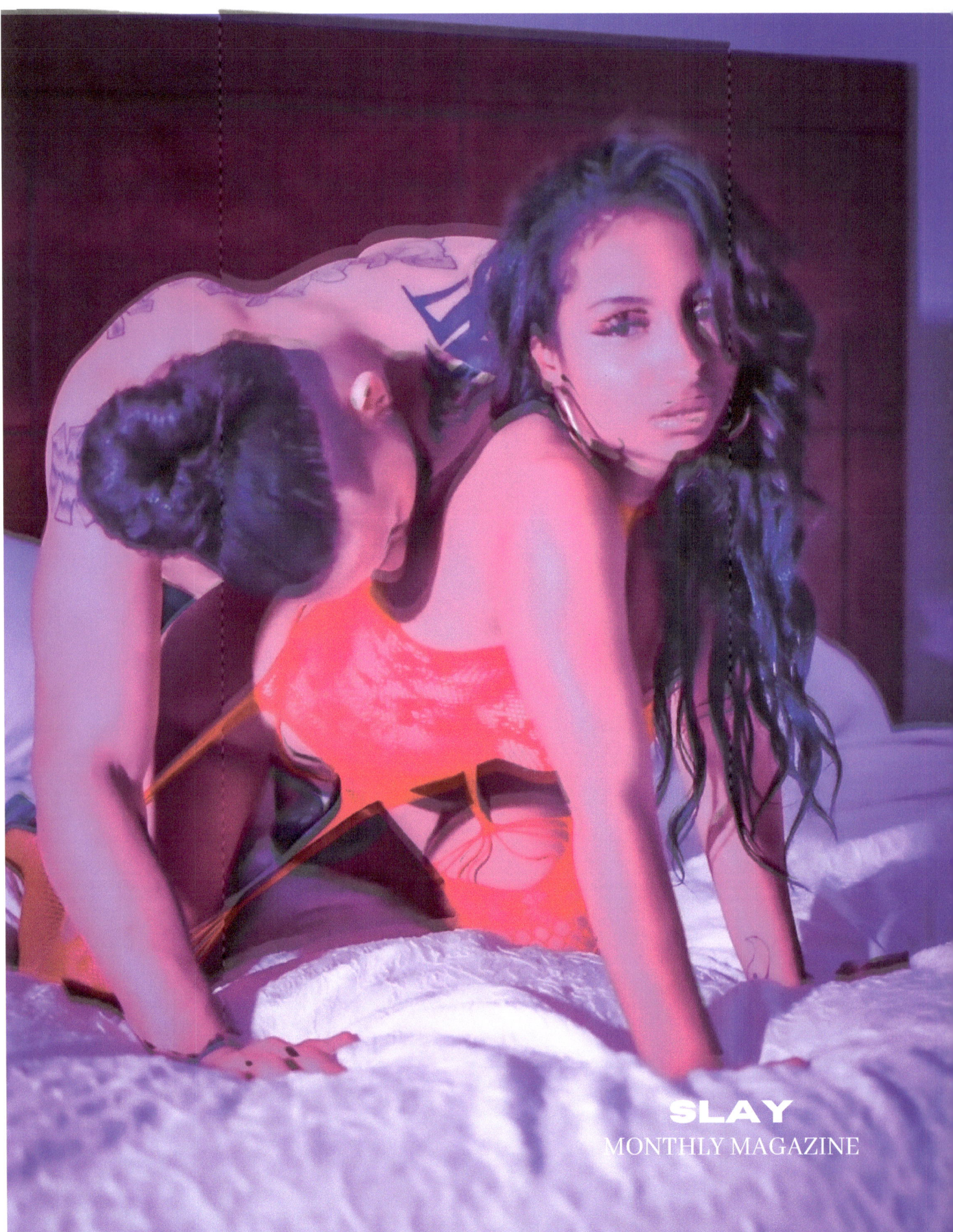

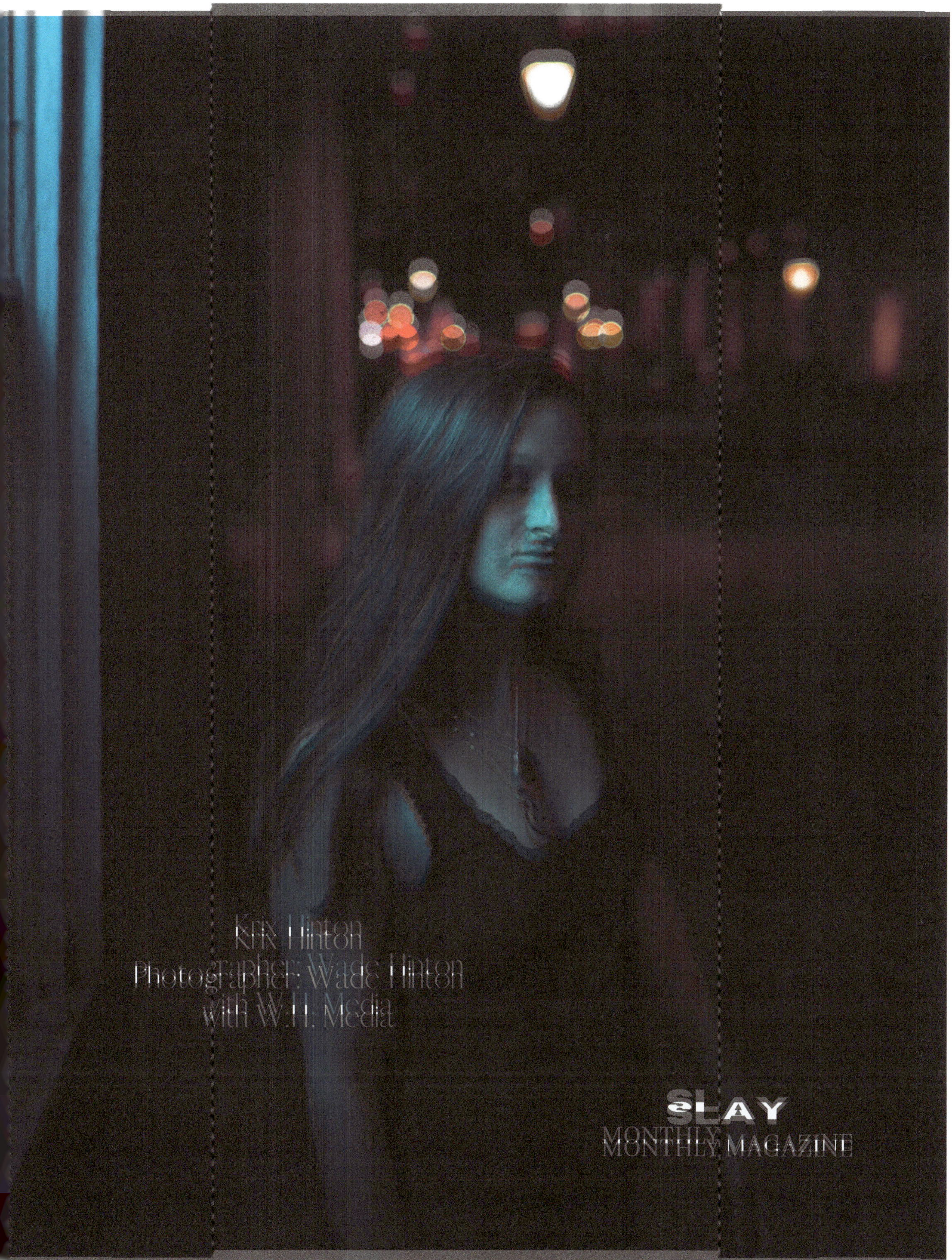

Krix Hinton
Photographer: Wade Hinton
with W.H. Media

SLAY
MONTHLY
MONTHLY MAGAZINE

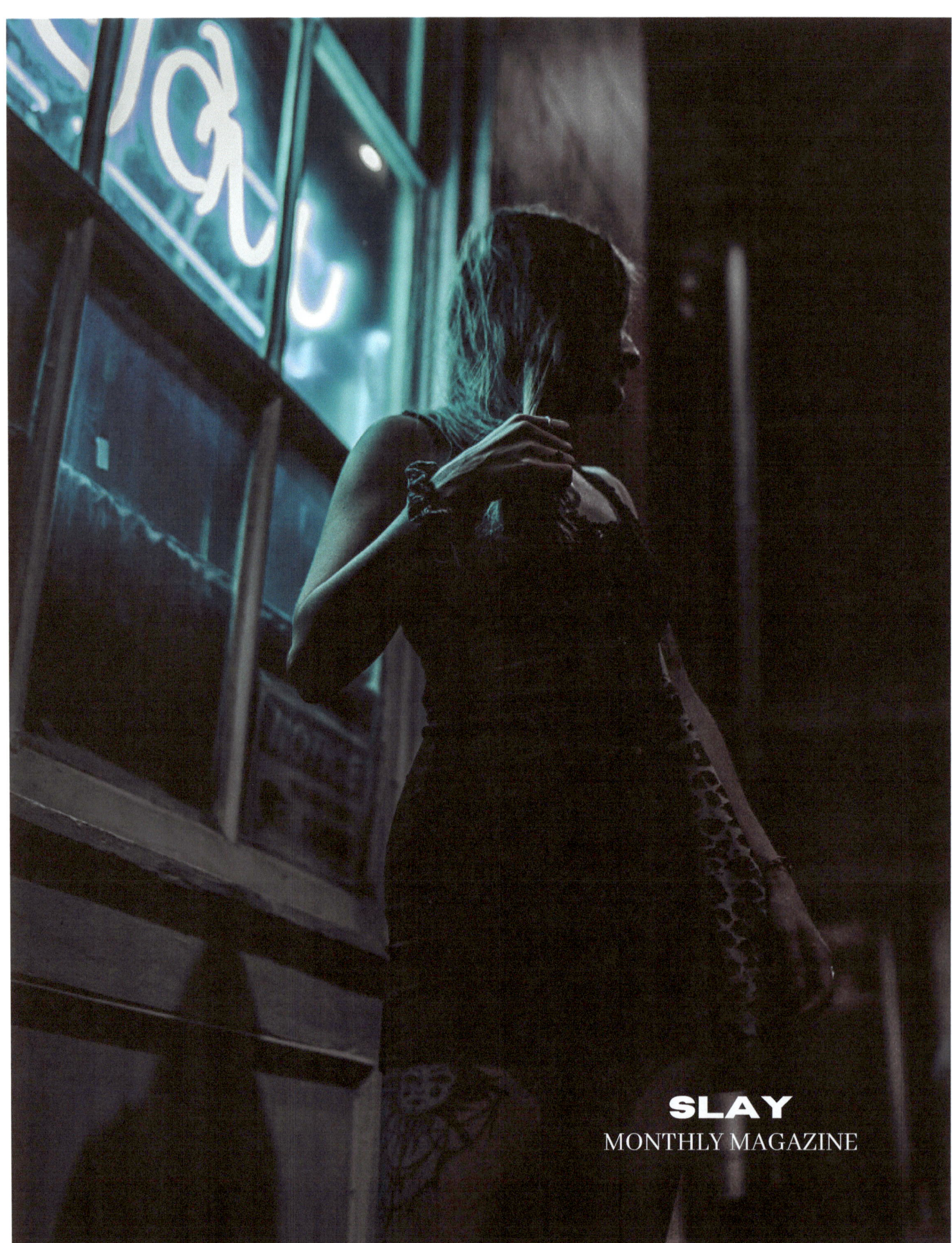

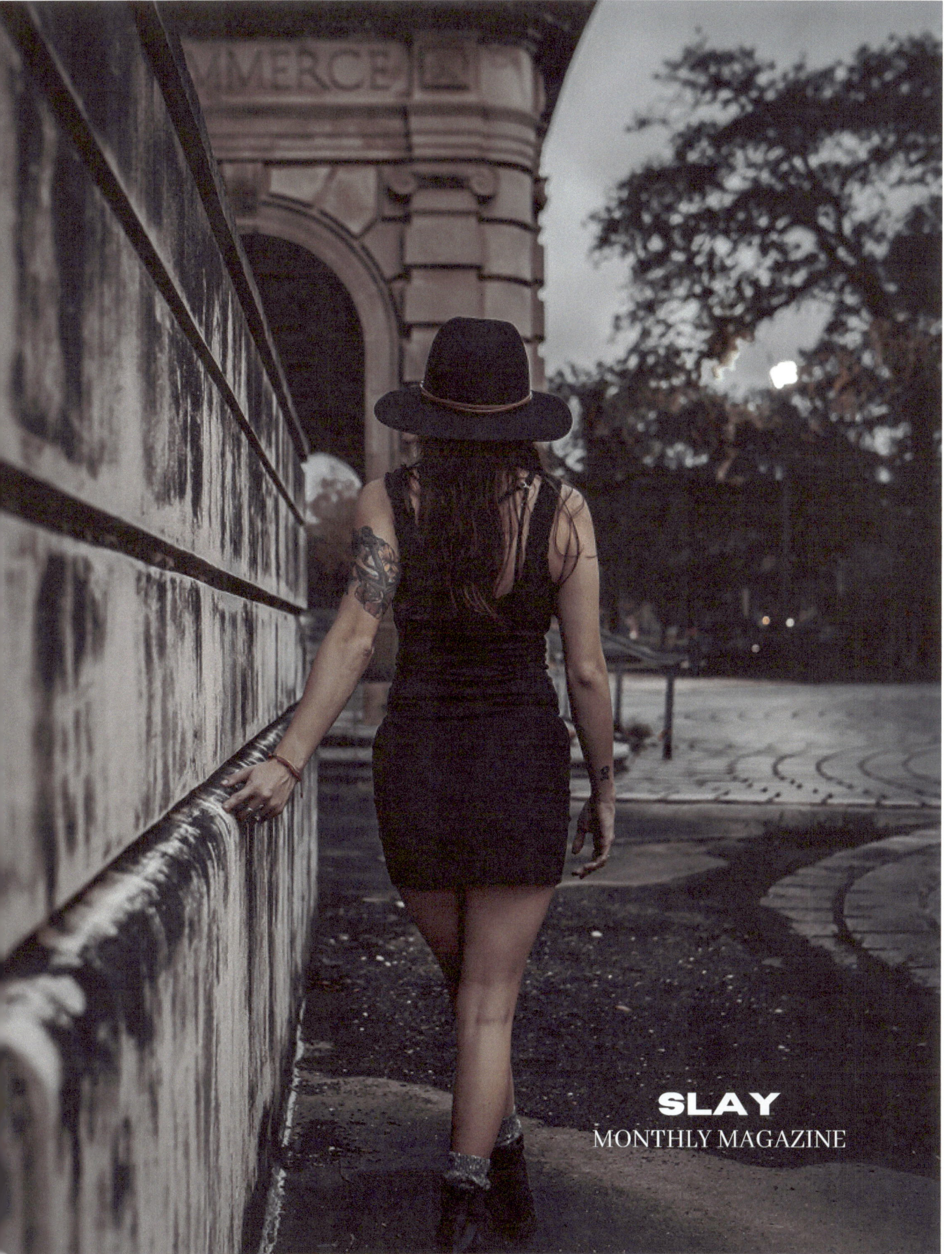

SLAY
MONTHLY MAGAZINE

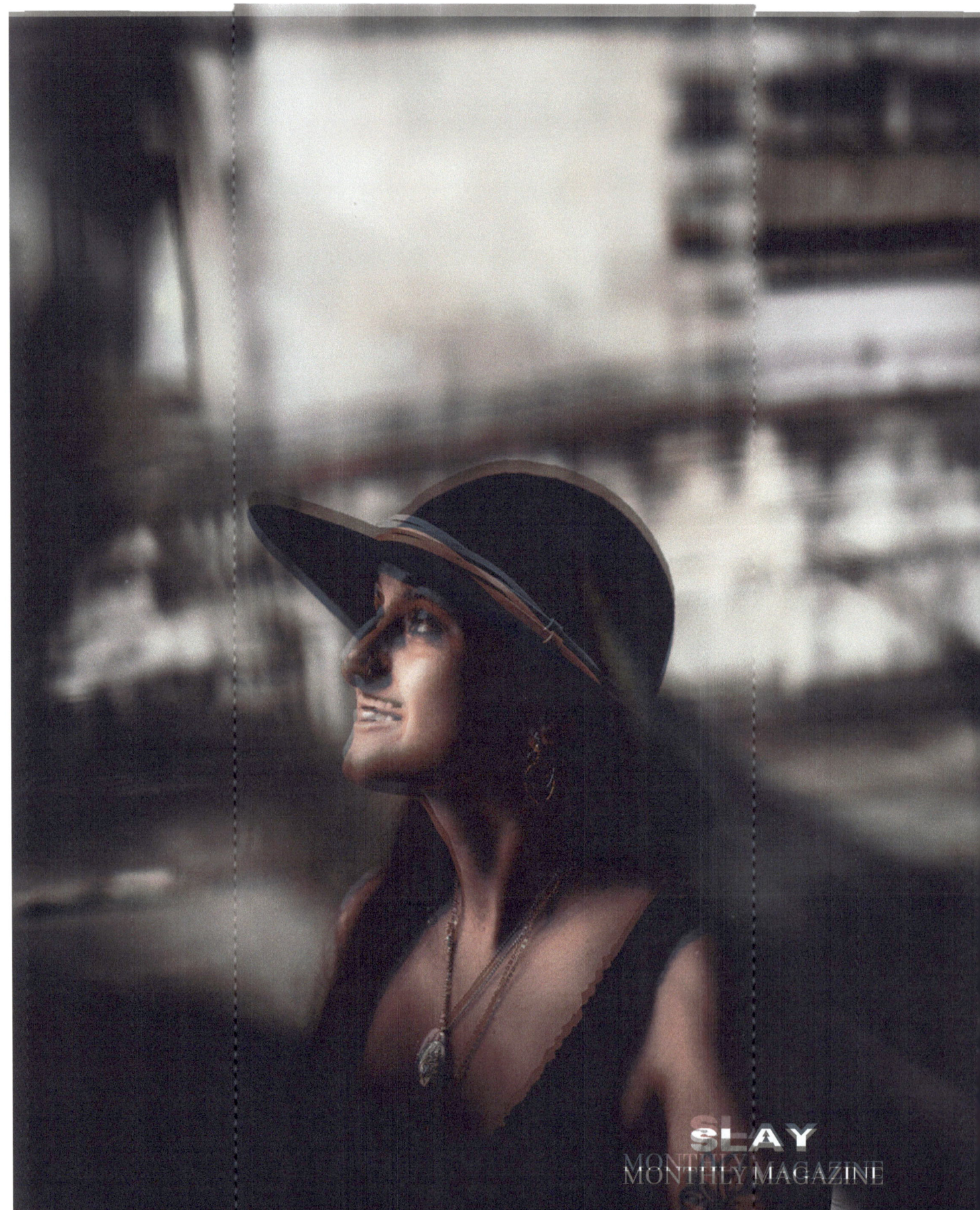

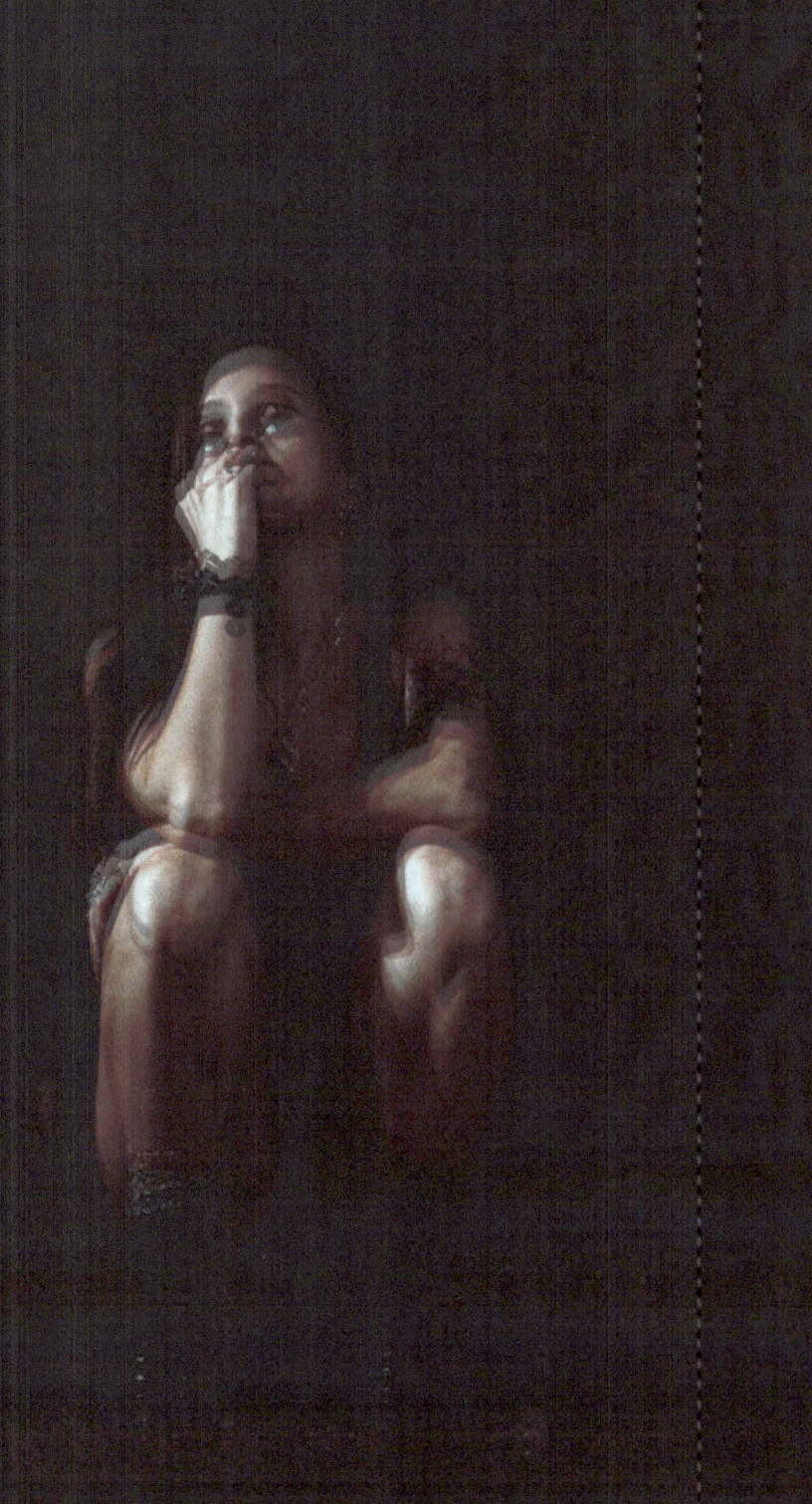

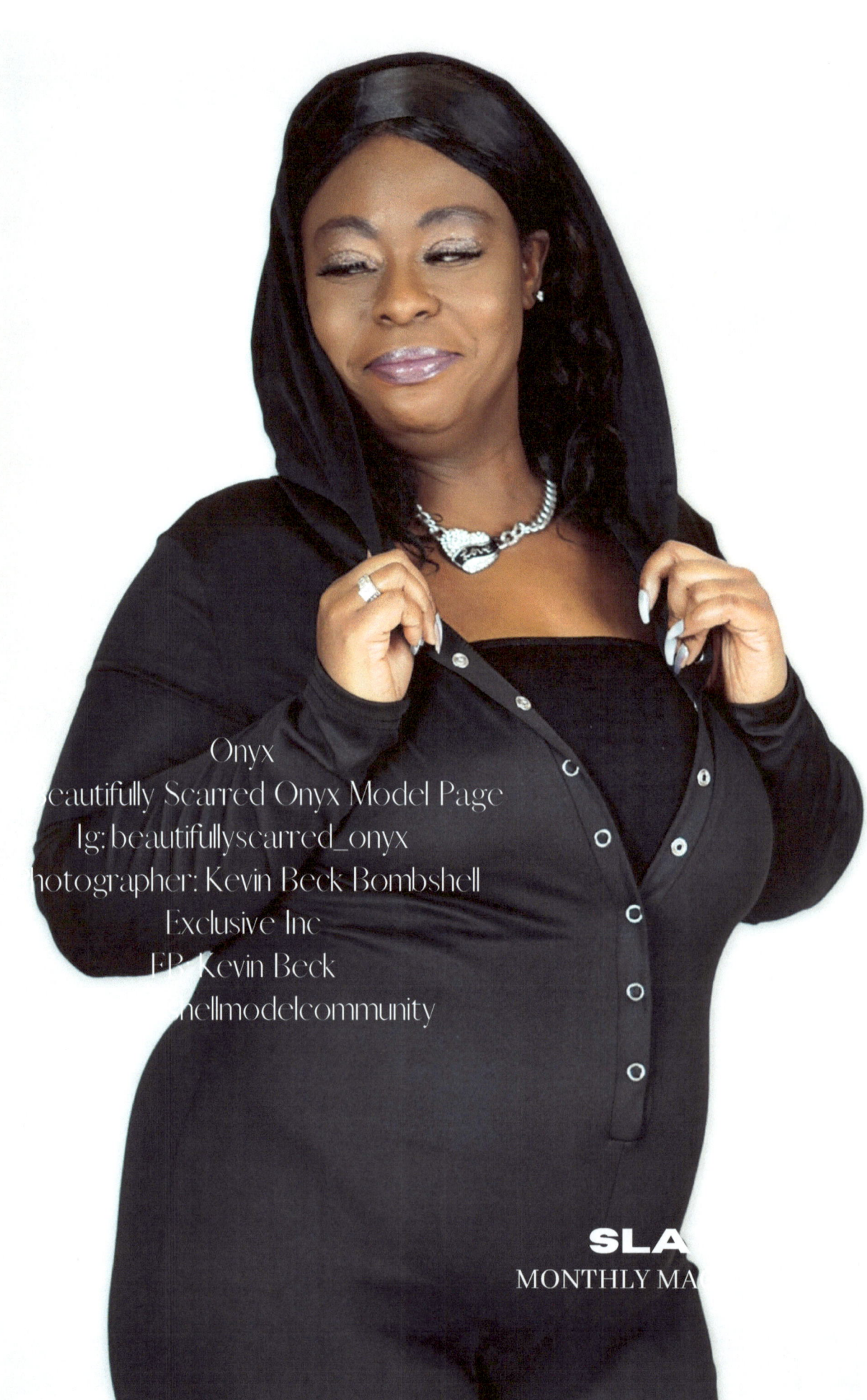

Onyx
Beautifully Scarred Onyx Model Page
Ig: beautifullyscarred_onyx
Photographer: Kevin Beck Bombshell Exclusive Inc
FB: Kevin Beck
bombshellmodelcommunity

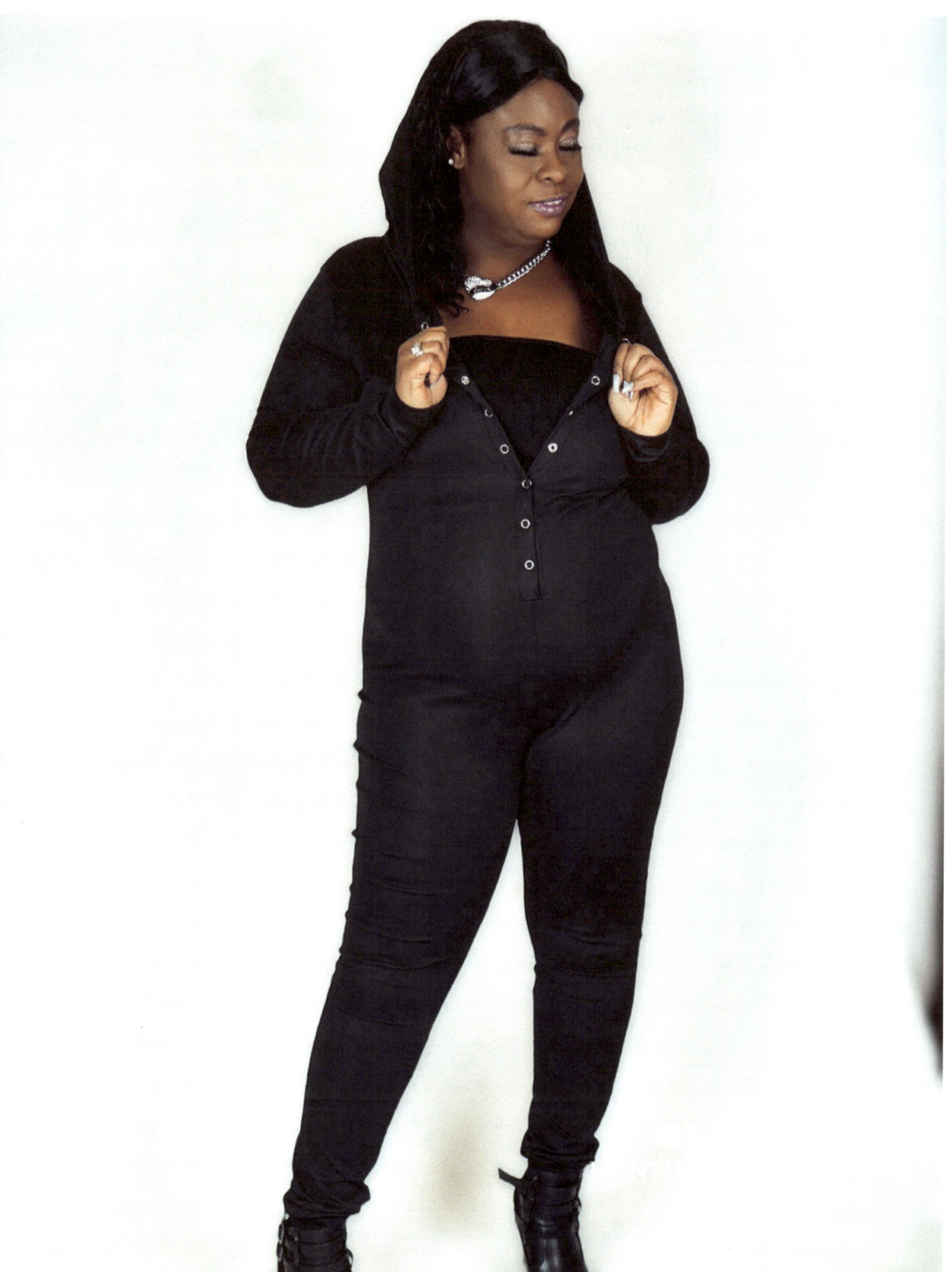

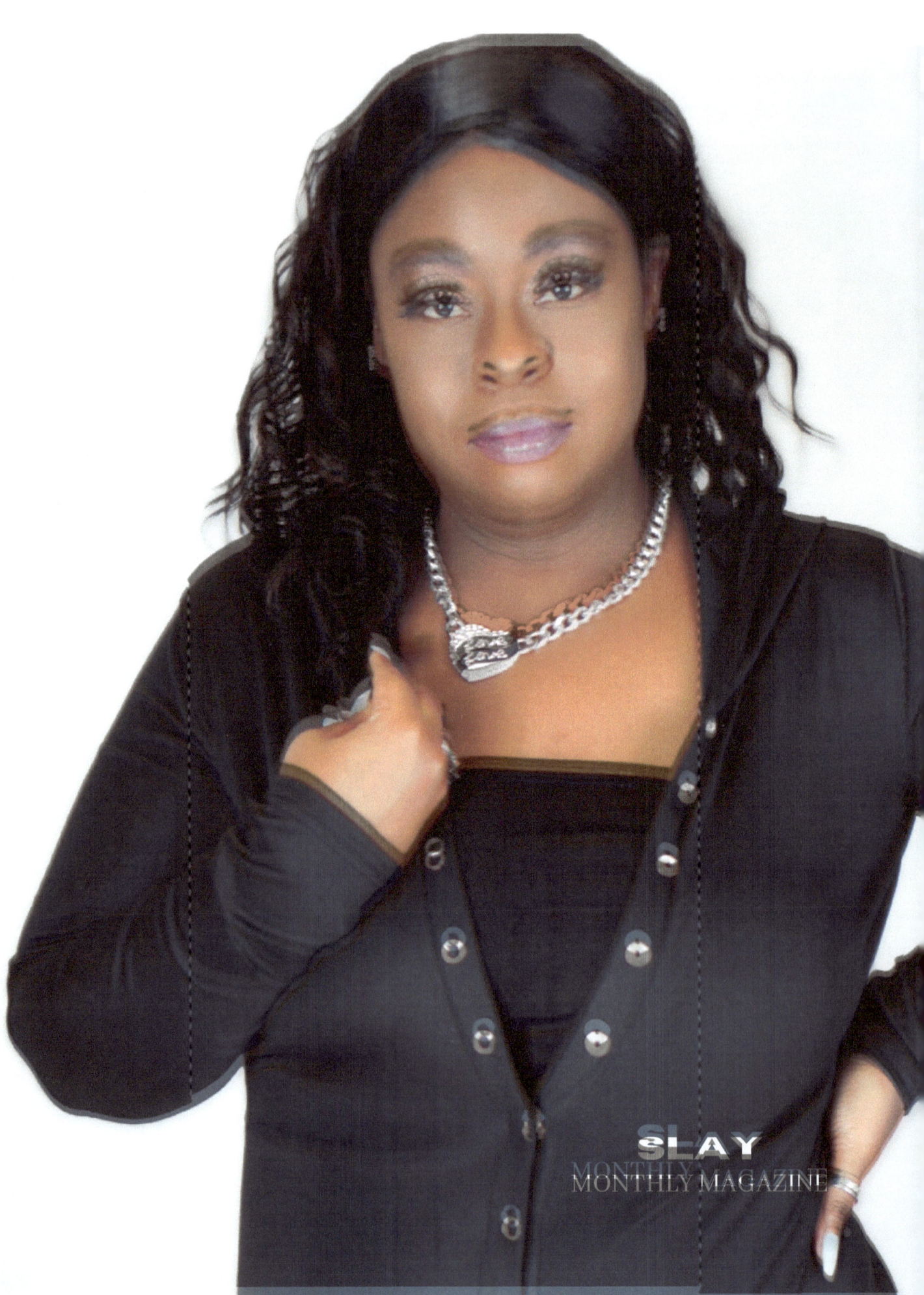

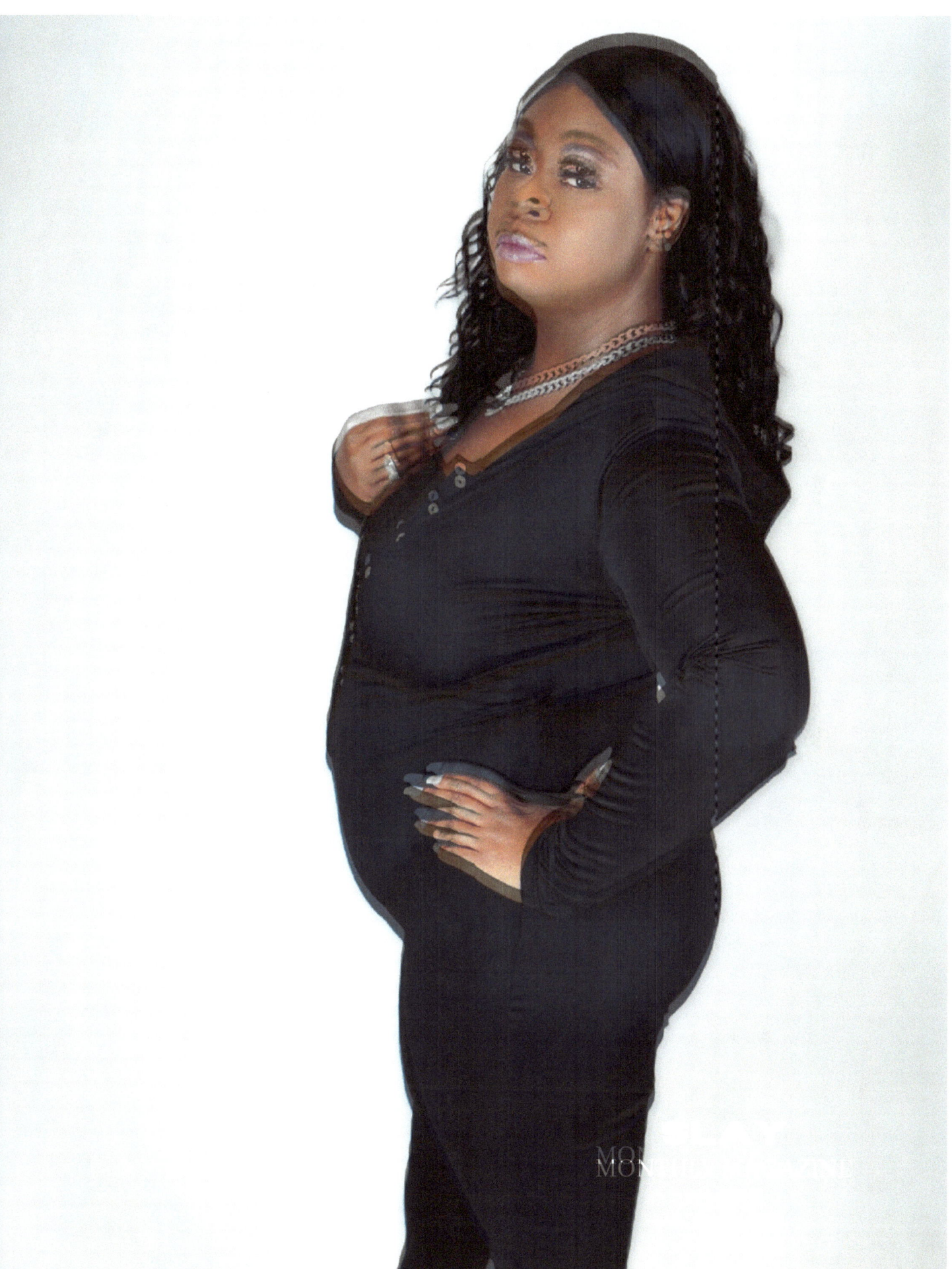

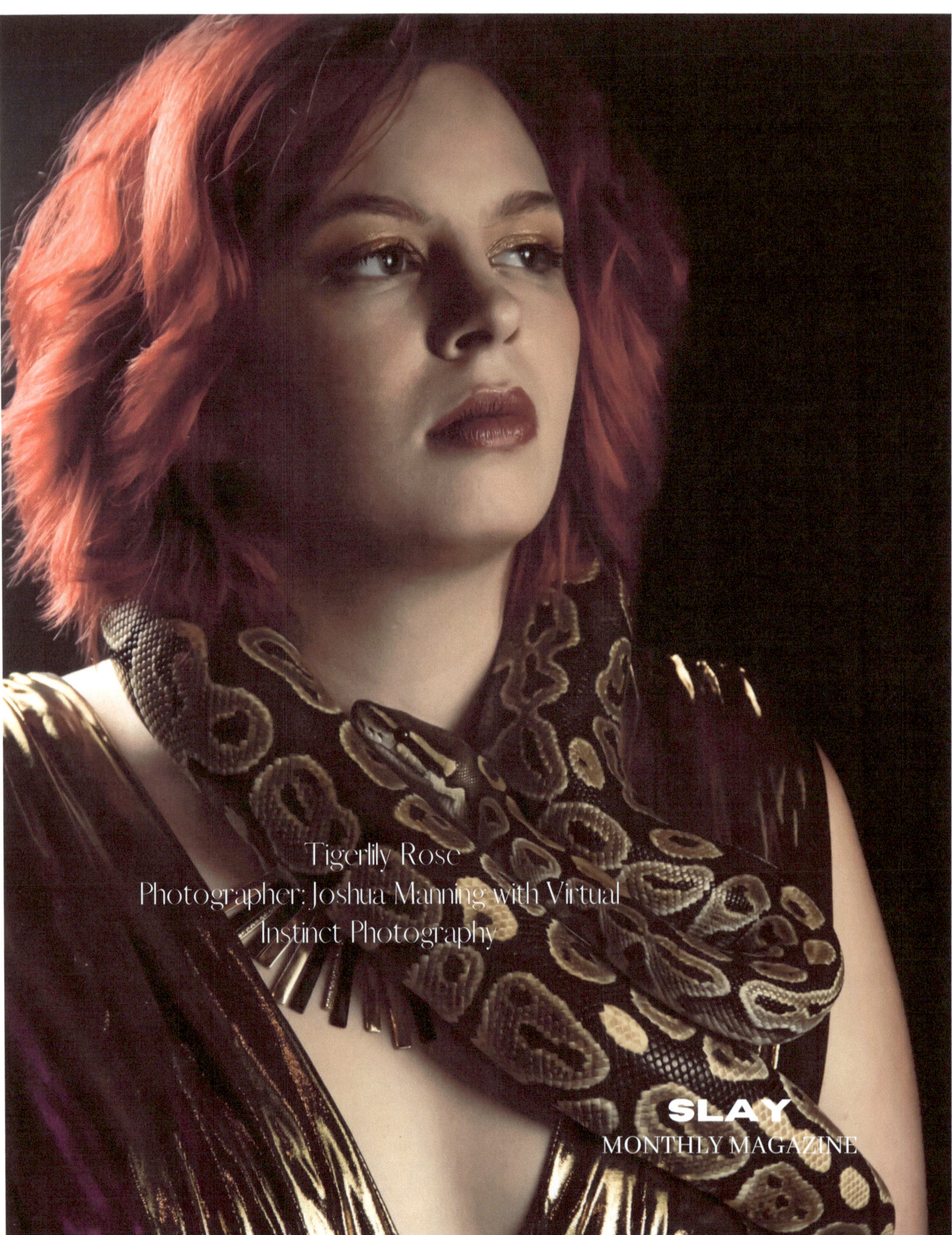

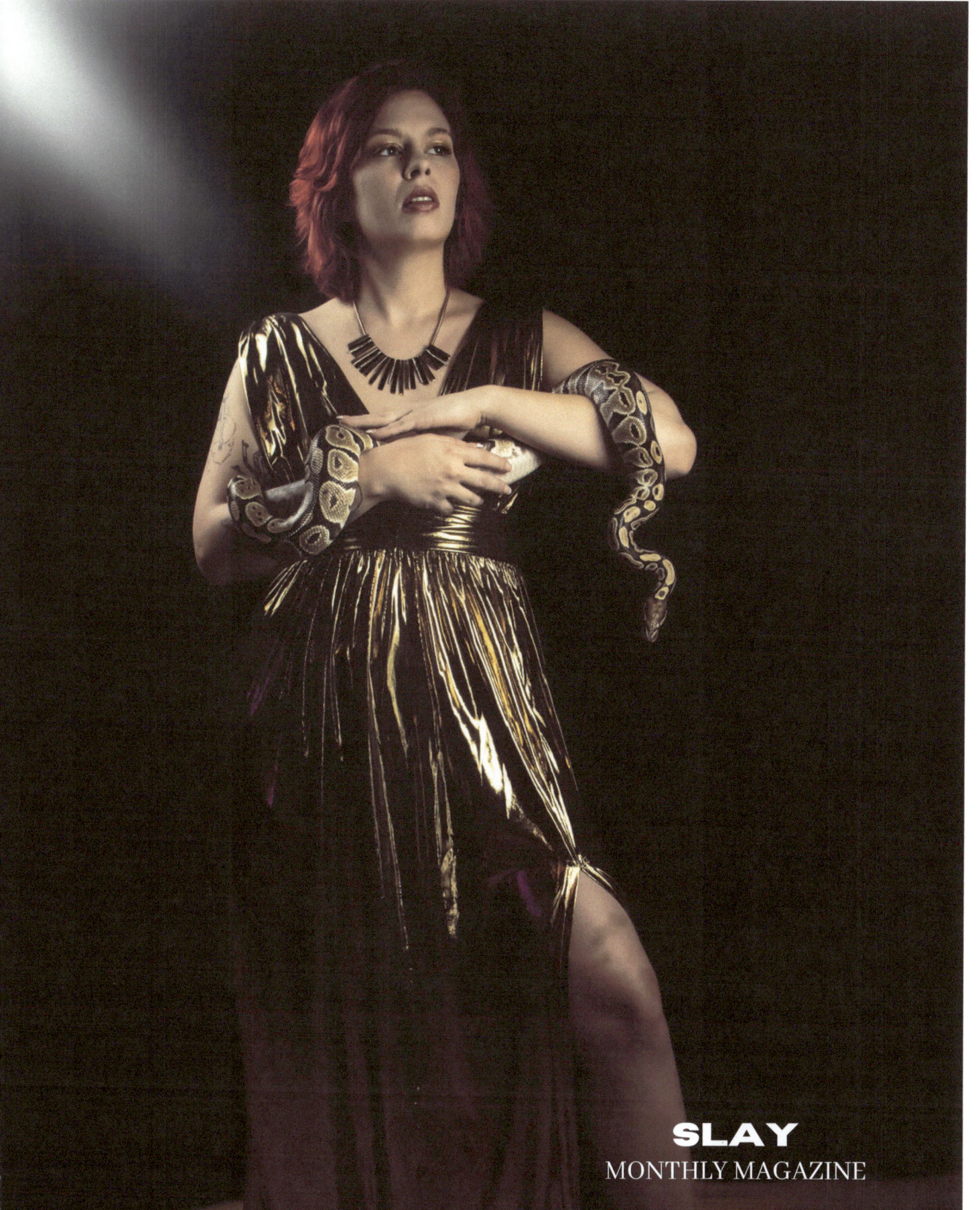

SLAY
MONTHLY MAGAZINE

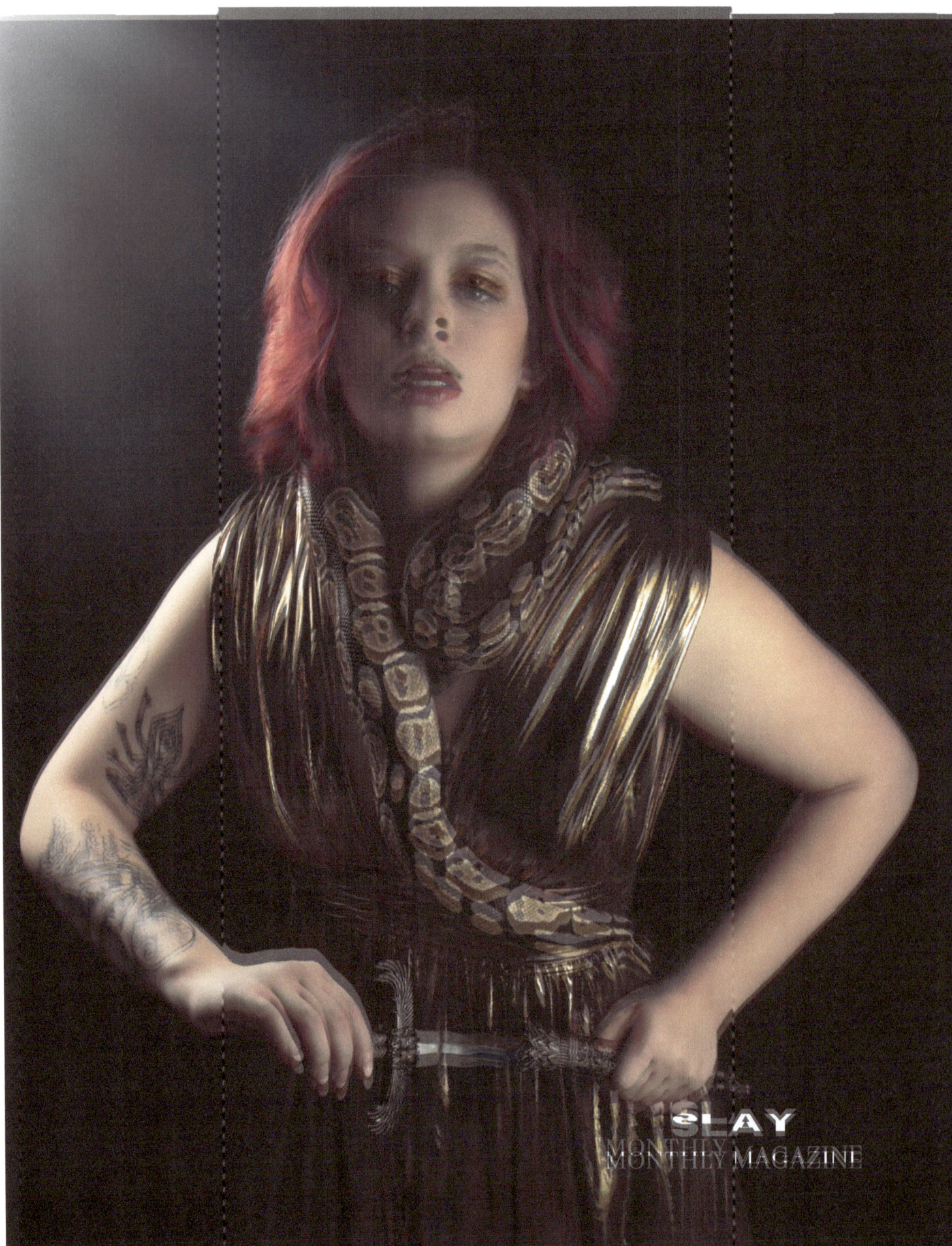

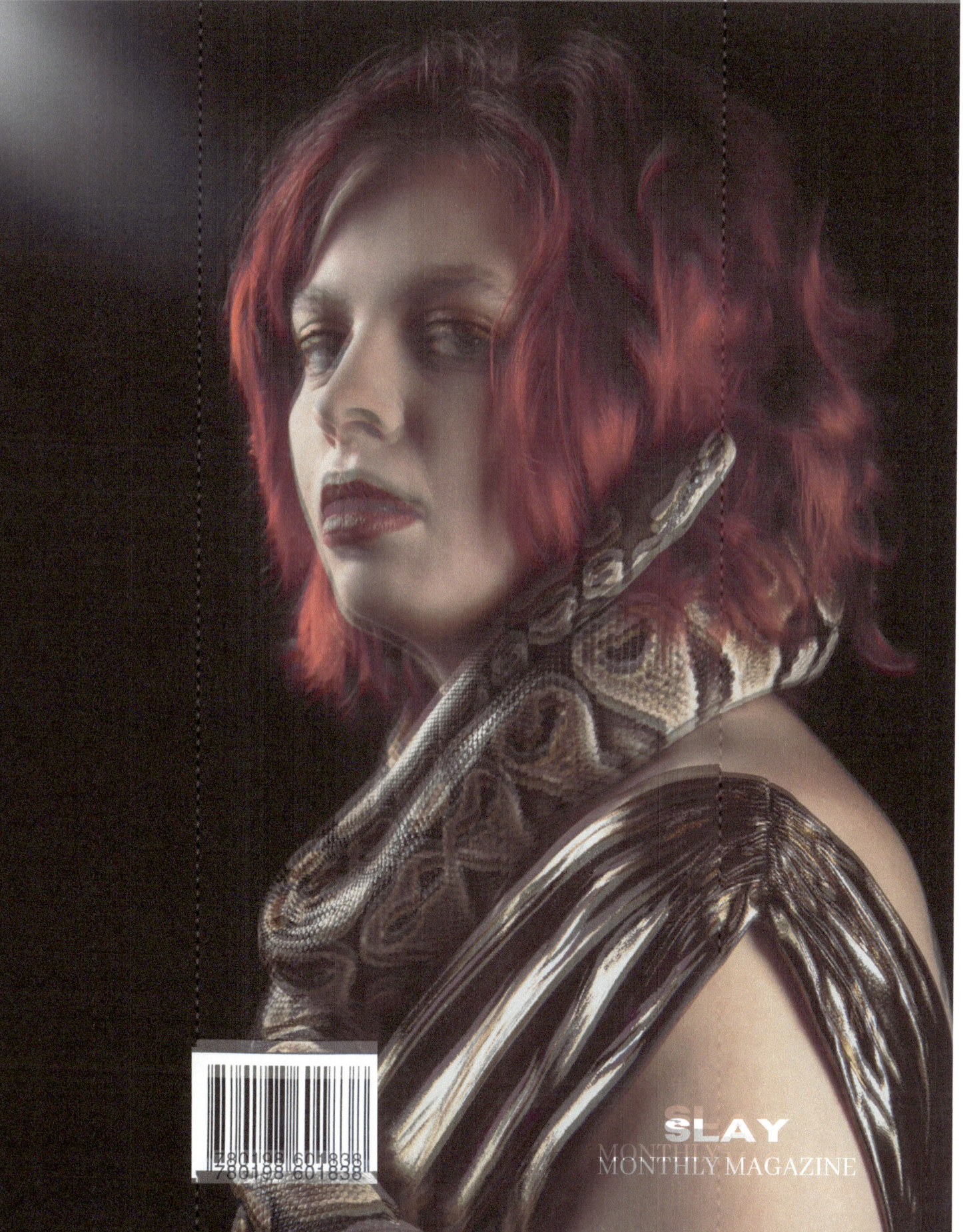

SLAY
MONTHLY MAGAZINE